The devil Almost Won, But God...

JOY MATHEWS

© 2017 by Joy Mathews

All rights reserved. No part of this book may be reproduced, stored in a retrieval system or transmitted in any form or by any means without the prior written permission of the publishers, except by a reviewer who may quote brief passages in a review to be printed in a newspaper, magazine or journal.

First printing 2017
Printed in the United States of America

Front & Back Cover Design by Kanika Harris
www.passionpgm.wix.com

Editor: Val Pugh-Love

ISBN: 9780692920220
Erica Joy Mathews Publishing

Dedication

I dedicate this book to my children starting with my oldest Antonious who everyone calls Scoota. Then, there's Je'Sika (not Jessica) who we call Pooh. Finally, there's Hailey who is my youngest. All three are the apples of my eye, and I wake up each day just to fight for them. They are my world, and I love them beyond measure. A mother's love for her children is like God's love for us when He gave His only begotten son Jesus to die on the cross for our sins. That is love!

Scoota, you know that I am with you no matter what, and I will ride with you until the wheels falls off. I am that female that will always be here, and I am that female that will keep it real with you no matter what. I am your backbone. If the day comes, and I am absent from the body, know that I am watching over you. I will always be in your heart. Never put your trust in man - they will fail you every time. I want you to get to know Jesus because He will be the only one that can keep you. I know from experience! I love you, son, and we were built to last. Stand tall!

Pooh, you know that you have always been my angel here on this earth, and I thank God for such a beautiful daughter. I want you to continue to blossom and flourish into the butterfly you are becoming. You're beautiful inside and out. I want you to know that God does things in His own way, and we do not always understand why He does what He does. But, it is always for our good. He will never put no more on us than we can bear.

Trust God no matter what! I need for you to pave the way for your baby sister and protect her just as I have protected all of you. I want you to always be there for your siblings because you will be their guide to staying strong. I want you to never give up and always press your way through. Even when you do not feel like it, press your way through. I love you, Pooh, and I am counting on you.

Hailey, you are my baby, and you are the reason my life changed. I wanted to be there for you and God knew exactly what He was doing when He blessed me with you. You helped me see through all my past failures, and you made me become a better mother. I had to step up to the plate and start taking responsibility. For that, I am grateful. I now have life more abundantly. I love you, baby girl, and I want you to know that you can do all things through Christ who strengthens you. I want you to always pray and remember that whatever you ask in Jesus' name, He will do it. (John 14:14) You just have to believe it. Love, Mommy.

To my parents, what can I say? I love you and am so grateful that I am your daughter. I could not have asked for better parents. Dad, thanks for sharing my grandmother. She is the reason I have this strength and faith in God. You both have been here for me throughout my life, and I know that I was not an easy kid to raise. The enemy was always trying to kill, steal, and destroy me. He did not want me operating in the gifts that God had given me, but God...Dad, you are truly the best, and we are truly better together. Never forget that! Your prayers, your encouragement, and your loyalty helped me conquer all my dreams, and I thank you for believing in me when I wanted to step out on faith and do the impossible. I love you, OH DAD.

    Mother, you truly stepped up when it appeared there was no hope. You gave me the comfort of knowing that I can trust you. I thank you for being that mother that would do anything for her child. I thank you for keeping the kids when I went to prison, and I thank you for your love. I thank you for moving in with me and taking care of me as if I was a small child. Your love made me strong. Mom and Dad, you are both jewels that have shined brightly. Remember, weeping may endure for a night, but "JOY" is coming in the morning. Only what you do for Christ will last.

    And, to my husband, Sederick. You really do not know how blessed I am to have you. You have had patience from the very beginning, and you continue to show me that patience. I know that I can be difficult at times, but you know that I mean well. Lol, you really showed me your love for me when I got sick. OMG…I could have never asked for a better mate. You set the record, and you showed me that true love does exist. You bring out the best in me, and whether you know it or not, you help me help myself.

    What do I mean by that? When I am out, I represent you. You look good, so I never want to make you look bad. You make me a better me, and you help push me into purpose. You support my vision. Thank you! You are amazing, and I did not know that I could ever love. However, you showed me that it was possible. It feels so good to love someone when they love you back. Thanks for not just telling me but always showing me. You are my rib. You were made just for me, and I thank God always on your behalf. I want you to know that I love you! Smile, My Superman!

A special thanks to Bernard Snowden, my dear friend that has supported me in all of my endeavors. I appreciate your continuous support and uplifting words of encouragement throughout out this whole ordeal. Most of all, I thank you for your patience and the love that you have shown my family and me. You are much appreciated, respected, and I truly love you, friend.

To "My Doctor Burton," I am so grateful that you have always spoken positively about the severity of me being diagnosed with Stage IV breast cancer, and later suffering from secondary malignant neoplasm of the brain having seventeen metastases located around my brainstem and cerebellum. I would like to thank you for never giving up on me and propelling to inspire that I would survive. Dr. Burton, you have always given me positive words to uplift my spirits, in my opinion, you are the best doctor in the world, and I salute you with the utmost respect and admiration. I am elated that God chose you for a special patient like myself.

Lastly, to my nurses Carol and Ashley thank you for going above and beyond for me. I thank the University Health team of Shreveport for having my best interest at hand. God knew exactly what I needed. Smile!

Introduction

Luke 1:37 says, "For with God nothing shall be impossible." We do not have to be strong or perfect. God uses our imperfections and our weaknesses to highlight His grace and power. I am here only to give you hope and to build your faith so that you can conquer all things. Jesus has already paid the ultimate price for you, and by His stripes you are already healed. Say it aloud: *By His stripes I am already healed.* Now, this time say it as if you are already healed. *By His stripes, I am already healed!* Wow! Do you realize that Jesus has given us authority to speak those things that be not as if they already were? The power of life and death are in the tongue. That means that I can have whatever I say that I can have, but the key is *believing* it.

Let me give you a brief description of strong faith. I was diagnosed with Stage IV Breast Cancer and was told that I had six months to live. Can you believe that I laughed in the face of the doctor? The enemy was using him to give me a bad report. I looked that devil straight in the eyes and said, "That is what you were taught scientifically, and that is okay. But, I am standing on what I was taught, and that is to trust God." So, there I was four weeks later, after having gone through my second chemo treatment, I had not gone through any pain nor was I taking any type of pain medication. I simply trusted God.

You're probably saying, "So what is your point?" That is where I am about to blow your mind. I AM ALREADY HEALED, and I am not waiting to tell you when the doctor gives me the report - whenever that may be. I am already giving you the report straight from the Father's mouth. (*For I shall live and not die...*) I am so excited that that is my testimony! Hallelujah! Thank you, Jesus!

All too often, we tend to give out medication to people, and we see that it works for them. Yet, when it comes to us, we tend to forget to use that same dosage. I have been operating in this gift since 2004, and it has worked mightily for others. I have seen the miracles that God has performed through me, and it has truly been awesome to witness. Now, did I ever think that I would have to speak over my own life and sickness that the enemy had brought upon me? No! Moreover, I had no idea of the faith that I have, and I am impressed, overwhelmed, ecstatic, and flabbergasted by it all.

Now here's the kicker, I recently prayed for this guy and his brother because they both were diagnosed with lupus, and they were so afraid. It is hereditary in their family and everyone has died from it. So, I called my elders up on the phone and everyone met me at my office to pray. I spoke life into their dead situation and stopped that generational curse right there at the root. Evangelist Barbara, Sister Pat, and I prayed for these brothers and fire from heaven came down and burned that disease and sickness away. We knew that God had healed them.

Later in the week, I received a call from one of the brothers saying that he had a good report. He told me he is healed (as if I did not already know). Months later, my dad saw him and told him what the doctor said about my health. Oh boy, he could not wait to get out of my dad's presence so that he could dial me up. My phone rang, and I answered in a graceful but cheerful voice.

"Hello."

He said, "Hey there! You sound great."

I replied, "I am!"

He said to me, "Your dad told me that you were diagnosed with Stage IV Breast Cancer."

I said, "Okay and your point?" He did not respond immediately, so I went on to say, "Did you not think that I wouldn't use the same medicine that I used for you and your brother? I AM HEALED!" He thought that I would be down, but little did he know, I AM already up.

Believe it or not

You will not believe that I took my third round of chemo on October 30, 2015. Oh, my God, it was a different experience. I first prophesied to a young lady that was only twenty-seven years old, and she was hurting from the inside out. I spoke to her straight from God's voice, and she confirmed that she knew it was real. Then, I headed to the treatment room and met an older lady who looked like she was one step away from giving up on life. She looked like death to me, so I spoke life into her dead situation. Before I knew it, I was laying hands on her. I told her what God told me directly, and she received it.

Now, I would like to share with you what God had described to me on that day while I was being treated. He told me that I was like Him, and He gave me the example of when He hung on the cross with the two thieves on each side of Him. He told me that He had no sin, and one of the men asked for forgiveness while the other did not acknowledge Him at all. Then, He told me I am cancer free and that I am only passing through to save lives and to bring sinners to repentance. Oh, my God, the words were so profound!

I finally understood why I am going through this. I am doing the work of Christ, and it is my faith that will see me through. Praise God for His awesome love. You do not have to ask me if I trust God, because by now you should know that I do. You should be building up your seed of faith, and it should no longer be like that mustard seed He gave to each of us. Start working your faith by doing and living it rather than just speaking about it.

Each trial and storm that you face isn't to tear you down. Instead, it is to get you prepared for the road ahead. Trust me, if you were not strong enough, God would not allow you to go through knowing you would fail. He does not set us up for failure, but for good success. Because I know this, each day my spiritual being gets stronger and stronger. The food that I consume daily is what has kept me. The word of God is so profound and nourishing to the body, mind, and soul. Get a dose and watch how you begin to overdose. This is a high that will not kill you; it will give you everlasting life. In fact, this word will be life for you. Now, say with me: *"If I receive this word with the spirit over the mind, this word will be life for me. I need life!"* Now receive it!

I took my fourth and final treatment on November 20, 2015. I felt like if I am healed, then why should I continue to do more treatments for something that will only continuously kill my good cells? I was done, and I did not need the approval of man when God had already spoken life into my dead situation.

Now, let me proceed by telling you that my family was hysterical when I decided that I was done with chemo - everyone except my husband who has supported me from the very beginning. He trusted that I had heard from God. Oh, and let me not forget my dad because he would have me rewrite this book and fix it. He has trusted God and His provision for my life. Nevertheless, my phone began ringing nonstop with a flood of questions. *Why are you going to stop taking your treatments? What did the doctor say? Do you think your decision is the right one?* I'd had enough of the naysayers. So when they would come to me with the negative talk, I would say, "Stop! I am healed and that is that. I do not need your opinions, and I definitely do not need your approval. Just watch my God work."

Our corporate fast at our church is on Tuesday. One Wednesday night at bible study, I was sitting in church and Bishop asked the congregation who had fasted that day. He asked for a show of hands, and four women raised their hands in response. He told them to come forward. He said that God had told him that someone had been on a fast that day and that he was so glad for their sacrifice. He then told the rest of the congregation to come forth, and we did. He gave the four ladies oil and had them to anoint each member in sections. He had them to repeat it seven times.

I know that about the third time around, I felt God heal my body completely from cancer. I was astonished as I stood there feeling the fire running through my body. It's a feeling that I cannot explain. You will just know it if it happens to you. Then, God told me, "You are healed." I started crying and praising Him for this miracle. He asked if I trusted Him. I said, "Yes," and He told me to run and thank Him.

I took off running fast around the church. After a few minutes, I came to a sudden stop because I was tired. *But God* commanded me to keep running, and so I begin again. When I finally stopped, I felt victorious. I felt like I could conquer the world with God leading the way. I was excited! Then, there was a part of me that felt loved, special, and definitely like daddy's little girl. I was the apple of His eye. An awesome feeling it was, and I knew that it was God that healed me.

When I got home that night I told my husband that I received my healing at church. He asked me, "Well, what about your back pain?" You see, the cancer had spread to my spine, and it was causing major pain. It was so bad that I had to use heating pads, and some days I was unable to walk. Still, my answer to him was he would have to ask God about my back pain. I told him that I did not know the answer to his question, and that I was only going by what God had spoken to me. I was healed! I did not care to hear more of the *what-ifs* and *whys*. Being healed was more than enough for me.

This girl has work to do! There's a passage in the bible from Luke 2:49 that talks about when Jesus was a lad and slipped off from his family to go into the temple amongst teachers who were astonished with his speech and answers. His parents searched all over for him. When they finally found him, they scolded him for running off without letting them know. His answer to them was, "Didn't you know that I must be about my Father's business?" Like Jesus, I have work to do!

I got a call from my friend Tresha about two weeks later saying that she would be in agreeance with my decision about not doing chemo any longer.

She said, "Girl, if you said God said it, then that is all the conformation you need." I thought that she was agreeing until she said, "But, what if it comes back?"

I told her, "It's not coming back.

She continued, "Okay, what if you start being in pain to where you can no longer walk again? Will you go back and finish the treatments?"

I said, "No."

"Well, why not?"

That is when God spoke to me clearly. "My child, you are healed. Do not ever doubt that. I healed you that night in bible study. Your back is simply a reminder. It doesn't hurt you, and you no longer have to take any pain medications for it. You do not have to use your heating pad, and you are back doing your daily activities. What you feel is a person that was once wounded and left with a scar. You're healed but simply left with a reminder. My child, I could have removed it completely, but I had to leave it with you as a reminder of what I did for you. If not, then you will forget."

My God knows His children and what we need at all times. Thank you, Jesus, for the thorn in my flesh as my reminder of the miracle that you, my God, my Daddy, my Healer performed. I told Tresha what God had just spoken, and it hushed her completely with no more questions being asked. My daddy had showed up on the scene when I least expected Him to do so and I cheered Him on. Now say it with me, "Go daddy! Go daddy! Go!" He loves when we give reverence to His Holy name.

On December 9, 2015, I had an appointment for my CAT Scan. I went - not because I needed an answer from the doctor - but just for my family and my book. If I had physical proof, people would not think I'm crazy, and then you guys could shout because the human doctor says it is gone. Anyways, I got it done along with bloodwork they do each time a patient comes to their office - the one thing I dread the most besides them messing with that port. (The port is an uncomfortable little gadget that's placed in the chest to make treatment easier.) I had a follow up the next day to see the surgical doctor. While examining me, he told me that the six-inch mass that was once there is completely gone and he could not even see where they had cut on me or performed the biopsy in three different areas. He told me that there was not a trace and that he wanted me to come back in three months just to be certain.

A few days after that, I went back to see my primary doctor for the results from the Cat Scan. When I got there, they wanted more blood. I was like I just gave blood on Wednesday, and I was not doing it again, so make Wednesday's blood work for today. The staff always laughs at me because they say that I am always giving everyone a hard time. (If you do not believe that, continue reading.) I went upstairs to see my doctor only to find out that I had a fill-in doctor because my primary doctor would be out until the next year. I was not thrilled when the fill-in doctor walked in the room to speak to me about something she knew nothing of - ME.

This lady knew nothing about me nor my condition other than what she was reading from my chart. She told me that my CAT Scan looked good and that my kidneys, lungs, bladder, and other body parts were not affected or damaged by the chemo. She said that everything looked great. These doctors are something else, because they never like to give God His credit by saying "You are healed. Only God could do this because we still haven't found a cure for cancer." The doctors cannot find a cure because God is in control. Wake up people, and trust God.

    The first step to defeating cancer is to trust God. You do not have to fall out, cry, and start claiming that you are sick and have cancer. You cannot start speaking negative things over your life. Instead, you must start fighting and claiming your healing. The bible states that there is life and death in the power of the tongue. If you say cancer has defeated you, then you will be defeated. You must speak life into your dead situation and trust God in every aspect.

    If you have skepticism, then I would suggest that you ask God to help you with your unbelief. I am sure that you are probably saying, "Well, that is what worked for you. My situation is much different." Let's stop right there because if you had no hope, then you would have left this book on the shelf and continued to wallow in your own mess of claiming a sickness that God did not put on you. However, you had enough sense to purchase this book in hopes of getting past this, too. You are now on the road to victory.

Chapter One

The Fight

Even when you are going through trials and tribulations, it is truly awesome to be serving God. I have learned to be content in whatever situation I find myself. God has everything under control, and He needs no help at all. We serve a God that will deliver us, and He has already won the victory. Because of this, nothing and no one can defeat us. It is not because we are mighty, but because of the God that we serve.

It is awesome when you show up in a boxing ring knowing you have already won the fight. You just have to show up and stay in the ring. *You just have to show up and stay in the ring.* Did I make myself clear enough for you? **You just have to show up and stay in the ring.** You cannot lie down. That means that you must not be afraid of the giants in your life - the ones that appear to be giants, the ones that make you back down, the ones that have you running, or the ones that take your focus off God and make you start focusing on the little g's or the present circumstance in your life.

The enemy wanted me to give up and throw in the towel. He thought that would have taken me out. He thought that blow would be the knockout punch since he had already thrown so many blows and caught me off guard so many times. Let me rephrase that, at least he thought I was caught off guard. I actually had on the whole armor because I was still standing and taking each blow that I was given. Each blow only drew me closer to God. God is my strong tower and my refuge in time of trouble. The enemy messed with the wrong one, and I was ready for the fight.

When the doctors told me I only had six months to live, I was not moved by their words because God had not spoken that to me ever. He said that I should live and not die. Therefore, I could not receive man's word in any form or fashion. The enemy wanted to take me out, but I did not have to worry about losing this match. I only had to show up and trust God no matter what the situation looked like. I had to stay in the ring and not allow the enemy to move me. He will try to trip you up. He will bring deception to you in every way. Nevertheless, you must be able to detect a counterfeit bill without having to look twice or second guess yourself. If it is not the voice of God, then it is counterfeit.

The enemy only perpetrates and disguises himself by being a carbon copy knowing he can and will never be the one true God. You may be broken by bad news, but trust God. I could not listen to the doctors when God had not spoken such to me. He is the creator of us all, and He is the only God that I serve and the only God that I fear. The bible says for us to fear no man. So, to me their words were not received in my spirit man because I truly trust God wholeheartedly. I want to get you to that place of comfort as well. I hope that when you are done reading this book, you will have either allowed me to plant the seed, or you will have allowed me to water it, and God will give the increase. Seed go! Seed grow!

Ephesians 6:10-13 says, "Finally, let the mighty strength of the Lord make you strong." Put on all the armor that God gives, so you can defend yourself against the devil's tricks. We are not fighting against humans. We are fighting against forces, authorities, rulers of darkness, and powers in the spiritual world. Put on all the armor that God gives. Then, when that evil day comes, you will be able to defend yourself. Moreover, when the battle is over, you will still be standing firm.

Chapter Two

Real Recognizes Real

    Let me give it to you raw and uncut. Looks are very deceiving. How would I know? I looked in the mirror many days, and I was good at what I did. Let me take you down memory lane so that you can see the tactics the enemy has set up for people. Now, do not think that I am reminiscing, I am simply sharing my testimony.
    I walked up to the steps and rang the doorbell. There was no answer, so I rang it again. Still, no answer. There I was standing on the outside of my grandmother's porch ringing the doorbell and not getting an answer. I began to have this eerie feeling in the pit of my stomach. The newspaper was still on the lawn, and she still had not arrived at the door to open it. I rang the doorbell once more before I start beating and beating harder. Still, there was no answer. I called my dad at work to let him know that my grandmother, which is his mother, has not opened the door. I was worried, and I just knew in my heart that she was gone.
    My dad arrived and tried to get inside, but the burglar bar door was secure. We did not have that key. Still, we tried and tried to no avail. Finally, he was able to break in somehow. I really do not remember how; I must have blanked out somewhere. I just know that we were able to get inside only to find her lying on the floor cold and asleep. She was gone to be with the Lord. I know some people are probably wondering how I know that. Well, it was not because she stayed in church, and it was not

because she prayed. It was because God had prepared her for that moment. She had her stuff laid out - keys, will, insurance papers, and every important paper we needed. It was laid out for us in plain view. That is how I know. I laid there crying and soon I became numb. I could not hear anyone; I had completely zoned out.

I was eighteen at the time. Although I was raised in the church, I did not know God personally for myself. So, I cried out and asked God to show himself to me. I remember sitting on the steps one night asking God to show himself. I remember telling Him that I know my grandmother knew Him. She often said His goodness and mercy shall follow me all the days of my life. She talked about how Jesus loved me so much and about all the things God had done in her life and for her. Now I wanted to know this God that she served. I wanted to be in that place of peace like her. She was such a wise woman of God - a virtuous woman of God. Her favorite saying was, "Weeping may endure for a night, but joy will come in the morning light. Troubles do not last always."

There I was in a place in my life where I needed to know God for myself. *Be careful what you ask for, because you just might get it.* I sat on that porch way past midnight and continued talking to a God that I did not know. I asked Him to move a star as I watched many of them in the sky. I told Him that if He was God to move that star, and I did not have to point at it. If He was God and He knew all things, He would know which star I was inquiring about. "Move it," I said. But, God did not move the star.

So, after waiting and waiting, I decided to get up and go into the house so that I could prepare for bed. I was laughing about God not showing himself and felt like he could not be real. And, if he was, I was not good enough for Him to move on my behalf.

My son was three months old at the time, and he was sound asleep. We called him Scooter Man because he started scooting at only two weeks. He was my baby, and I loved him so much. I was roommates with my childhood friend, and this was our first home outside of our family homes. I had a mattress but no bed. There was no central air and heating. This was the month of December, so it was very cold. I had a space heater in my room. I laid down for bed only to be awakened at 3:23 a.m. I had one of those clocks that lit up in red. I looked at the clock and down at my son only to find him not lying on the mattress.

I looked at the space heater, and my baby was sound asleep under it. I immediately snatched him from under the heater and got burnt in the process. He was still sleeping, and he was not hot nor was he burnt. God had covered him that early morning. It was my first encounter knowing that God was real. I said, "God, I will never try you like that again." God showed me that he was indeed God and God all by himself.

I was raised in the church since I was a baby and had been taught the word from the very beginning. The first scripture I learned was John 1:1: "In the beginning was the word and the word was God and all things were made by Him." I would go on quoting the rest of the verses. I did not know that the seed had already been planted and was being watered. But God... The bible says to train up a child in the way they should go. Believe me, my grandmother did just that.

I thought that we churched entirely too much. I thought that when I got grown, I would do away with the church thing because I was burnt out. I was sick of church and all the hypocrites that came with it. I was tired of the ones that said, "Hallelujah! Thank you, Jesus!" inside church and cursed right after. I was already gifted with the spirit of discernment. I just did not know this was a spiritual gift at the time. I did not know that God was preparing me at an early age, even in my mess.

My pain was my gain, and my weakness became God's strength. My faults, my failures, and my mistakes were all for His glory. That is my testimony for God's people. Those things were what brought me to exercising my faith. I encourage each of you to exercise your faith daily. You have to trust God in all that you do. Do not look at the problem; rather, focus on the solution (God). He is the solution to every problem. I have done everything under the sun. Today, I can say I am delivered and set free. John 8:36 says, "If the son sets you free, you are free indeed." I had praying grandmothers who interceded on my behalf. Thank God for prayer. Thank Him for the anointing.

What can wash away my sins? Nothing, but the blood of Jesus! You may be wondering why that is important. Faith is good because it moves God. However, the blood is what covers you. The blood covers your household, job, sickness, issues, sins, and you as a whole. It is the blood of Jesus, and I want you to grab hold to that. Stop right here and meditate on the blood. It will never lose its power. It was the blood of Jesus. He paid a debt that He did not owe. He suffered and died on the cross just for you and me. The blood! The blood of Jesus!

By the time I was twenty-one, I had two children - a boy and a girl. Scooter and Pooh is what I called them.

They were my pair. My saying used to be "two and I'm thru." My patience was very short, and I had no time for keeping them. I wanted to treat them like my dolls - dress them up and make them look good only to throw them back on the shelf.

I was neglecting my children without even knowing it. I thought I was being a good mom. However, I was in and out of jail and catching charges like it was a disease. I was selling crack cocaine, shoplifting, printing checks, writing checks, stealing cars, and more. You name it, I have done it. The only thing that I have not done was drink alcohol or smoke drugs. I tried marijuana in my early twenties, and I was tripping like Craig on *Friday*. I could not handle it, so I did not do it again. I knew that was not for me. When it came to drinking alcohol, I did not like not being fully alert to what was going on around me.

While there was no drinking and no drugging, that did not stop me from selling it. I sold much crack. When people saw me, they did not expect that I was a queen-pin unless they knew me and I was rowdy, cunning, and working for the devil. The spirit of deception was activated and working in full affect. See when the enemy is using us, we tend to be unaware of it. We do his work, and we get charged with his foolishness.

I caught charge after charge because of this cunning manipulative devil, and I was the one who had to live with it. But God… What the devil meant for my bad, God worked it for my good, His purpose, His glory, and His promise. My mess is what gave me faith. I was exercising my faith each time I faced an obstacle. Build your faith on your problems, and soon you will trust God without hesitation. It will become natural, and you won't have to practice it. You can simply live it.

Time was passing me by so quickly, and I was willingly living in sin. I thought the life that I was living was *the life*. I did not know that it would send me to prison and away from my kids on a five-year sentence with the feds. When you are doing federal time, you have to do eighty-five percent of your time. I was so not ready for that. At the time, I was real hard and time was not about to get the best of me. I made up in my mind that I did the crime, and so I had to do the time. The feds were so pissed off at me for not ratting on the people who were involved in this scam that they sent me to Tallahassee, Florida. That was extremely far from Shreveport, Louisiana, and there would be no way that I could see my kids. If I did see them, I knew it wouldn't be often.

There I was doing time, and it was not worth it at all. If I could take it back, I would. It was too late, but that was what brought my faith about. My back was against the wall, and I was sick. My heart ached, and no one knew the pain that I felt inside. So, I began praying and calling on a God that I hardly knew. I needed Him then more than ever before, and I needed Him fast because I was about to lose my mind. God really shows up on the scene right in time and gives you comfort that you cannot see. You just know it is there, and it embraces you in a way that no man can. He calmed my fears and started speaking to my heart. It was much needed because I had time to do, and it was only the beginning.

I stayed in Caddo Correctional Center in Shreveport (CCC) for over a year before getting shipped off to the federal prison. It was a place that I needed to be.

The one good thing that I could say about being there was they had church every day - some days, two and three times a day.

A church lady name Sister Ealy would come once a week to preach. That is when everyone would come out their cells to hear what word she had for that week. She was so hood, but she was surely connected to the spirit of God because she could tell you things about yourself that only you and God knew. She called CCC "The Choice, the Challenge to Change." It was entirely up to you if you wanted to leave that place knowing and serving a God that could keep you from falling. You had a choice, and she was there to spread God's word in truth.

At the time, I did not know anything about spiritual gifts and that she was gifted with prophecy. I just knew that I was drawn to her spirit. It was not because she could tell me about hidden secrets or my past that God revealed to her. I was drawn to her because I was seeing my gift operating through her. I just did not know how to activate it. She was not the only one coming to give God's word and spreading the good news about a Savior that I had no relationship with.

I thought that it was nice for the people to take time out and come to visit the prison because some people had no one and no support system. They were alone, and to me that was hard time. I was grateful to have had my mother and father. I was also grateful that my mother had both of my children raising them until I was done serving my time. I was very fortunate, because some women did not know where their kids were. Some were in state custody, and some were with strangers, which caused more stress on that individual. I thank God for keeping mine together and with family.

I yearned for God's love daily, and I started opening my bible and asking Him to come into my heart and change me. I wanted to be better, but the enemy had been deceiving me for so long that I did not know how to be good nor did I want to live right. I have to tell you that when you are messed up, God has work to do - and I do mean work. However, you must be willing and ready for God to make you over again.

It took about six months for me to want more of God. I had been at CCC, and I was studying the word daily. I was in school learning and some days were harder for me than others. Some days I would curse people out. Other days, I would fight. Then there were the days I simply didn't want to read God's word. This was not because God was not making me over, but because I was so messed up inside. He had some serious work to do. That is just my personal belief.

One day, He told me that I would have to start staying in my cell to stay separate from spirits that were destroying my growth. I was obedient and stayed in. I would come out only to use the phone, which was not often. I ate in my cell, I bathed in my cell, and God was molding me day by day. I stayed in that cell for ninety days, and when I came out, I had word in me. I felt like I could conquer the world. I was so full of the spirit of God. I was so excited. Because I was a babe in Christ, He made sure no one brought danger my way. God made sure that I did not receive word that was false or that was not lining up with His word. I had a daddy that truly loved me, and I could rest in Him knowing that He would protect and keep me.

My faith was truly beginning to grow. Hebrews 11:1 says, "faith is the substance of things hoped for, the evidence of things not seen." This was a scripture I quoted daily, and this was what activated my faith. I had to start believing and trusting God's word, because the bible states that it is impossible to please God without faith. So, I had to start exercising my faith by putting it to work. God had really begun using me in that place. The inmates started seeing the light in me, and then the guards began to see it too. It seems like people are good at pretending and can fool some people. However, when God does a new thing inside you, you cannot help but shine. They know it is real, and they cannot deny it.

So, there I was operating in the spirit and God was truly using me. I was prophesying over people's lives, and God was bringing things to pass. Whenever people saw the evidence, they would draw closer to me and wanted to know what the Lord had said about their lives. I was truly on a high, and I was enjoying the ride - even from jail. I'm grateful that I went, and I am grateful that I found Jesus straight from a jail cell. Hallelujah! Some people never find Him because His word says to seek Him with all your heart. That is what I did; I knocked and He answered the door for me. Praise ye the Lord. I am forever grateful.

The Lord was building my spirit man up and preparing me for the day that I would be getting shipped off to Tallahassee, Florida. I called that federal prison facility Sodom and Gomorrah. It was truly a wicked place, and the people were lost. I hated the day that God allowed me to fall in the mouth of a lion only to eat me alive and kill all that was built up on the inside of me. I went in forgetting the word and allowing those demons to invade my space. I gave in to the devil and his army. It was an army of many, and they were killing, stealing, and trying to destroy you if you weren't batting for the same team as they were. I went in thinking that I had this under control and forgot about the God that brought me to this point. I got puffed up within myself and got taken out in the first round.

Now, do not get me wrong… I was still reading my word. However, I was not doing bible study, and there was not as much church as there was at CCC. At this prison, the inmates had to work and did not have all the leisure time that was allowed when I was in the county prison. It was hard, and again I was surrounded by homosexual acts that went on all day every day.

I had been there for almost two years when God spoke to me. I was laying on my bunk when God asked me if I trusted Him. I told him I did. Then, He told me to get up and go to the drug program to get into the class so that I could go home eighteen months early. I told God that the class was full so that disqualified me. In addition, I did not have a drug history listed in my file. Moreover, it was simply impossible.

He spoke to me again and asked if I trusted Him. Again, I told Him I did. He told me to get up and move. So, I did! That was not the first time God had instructed me to do things and they came to pass. However, that was the first time He worked on my behalf. Let's just say this was something just for me. It was something to build my faith for the day that cancer would try taking charge over my body. This was what I did not know, but God knows all. He was simply preparing me for the road ahead. Faith! That would be the only thing that would move God on my behalf. So, as God instructed, I jumped up and ran to the drug program to speak to Dr. Marcelis. I told him that God sent me and that I had to get in the next class. However, he told me everything that I told God while laying on my bunk.

There was no way possible I could get in the class, and it would have to be an act of God. "No way, no how," he said. Still, I wouldn't budge. I just sat there, and that is when he asked if I had someone that could write a letter from outside to vouch for me. I needed a job that would send a letter on my behalf and that could possibly get me into the next class which would be nine months later. The class that was beginning was already full, and they would be moving in the very next day. I got up and said, "Thanks, I will call my dad to get everything faxed over. I am believing that God is going to do it for me now and not later." He then said, "It would have to be a miracle." I replied, "It will be because God said it." I got up and walked out on that note, trusting God.

As I headed back to the dorm to call my dad, I was operating in faith. I called my dad and told him what had to be done for me to come home early. He got on it quickly. He had human resource to type a letter on my behalf and fax it over to Doctor Marcelis. The next morning, I got up and headed back to the drug program to see if he received the fax. However, he was not in and would not be because he was out with his sick daughter. I was thinking *oh boy* as I gathered this info from the secretary who was not supposed to share the confidential information of an employee. I left with my head down. Yet, when three o'clock came and no one's name was on the call-out to move over into the drug program, I sighed with relief and hope. I was now waiting until Monday for the doctor's return. *This will be a long weekend,* I thought to myself.

    Finally, Monday arrived. I got dressed and headed to see if Doctor Marcelis was back at work. I made it to the drug program, and he was there. His daughter being sick had everything to do with God's plan because if he would have shown up to work on Friday, I would have been out of luck in getting into this program. He told me that he had gotten the fax and that I would be coming into the program. I was ecstatic! As I got up thanking him, he told me that I was right and that God had to have worked that out because that was a miracle. I laughed and headed to the door with my head held high. I was so overwhelmed with excitement, and I rushed back to call my dad with the great news.

    I was heading home in nine months, which was eighteen months sooner than my actual release date. I could start preparing myself for the world that I would soon reenter. I was ready, so I started equipping myself by putting on the whole armor of God. He was truly working in my favor, and all I was striving to do was keep Him with me the day I was set free. You see, a lot of people go to jail and act as if they have changed. They quote a thousand scriptures and when it is time to go home, they leave Jesus at the gate and forget about Him. Then, they go back to the life that they were living - the life that only prepares them for hell. You have to realize that we all have choices. We can choose to live right, or we can choose to rebel against the will of God for our lives. You must choose life!

I know for some people, it is hard to put your trust in something that you cannot see. I understand that, but think about this. We put our trust in man and man lets us down over and over again. Man lies to us, and man fails us each and every time. So, if you have tried man, then why not try Jesus? This time you will find out that He sticks closer than a friend. He loves us dearly, and it was He who made us and not we ourselves.

Show me your faith, and I will show you my faith by my works. Faith without works is dead. It is impossible to please God without faith. I encourage each of you to start denying yourself daily. I encourage you to pick up your cross and follow Jesus. I encourage you to just trust God. I encourage you to believe God for His word. The word is truth and everything that is written has already been and will become. Nehemiah 8:10 tells me for the joy of the Lord is my strength. I look to Him in all that I do and go through.

Chapter Three

Building to Stand

"But, by the grace of God I am what I am: and His grace which was bestowed upon me was not in vain; but, I labored more abundantly than they all: yet not I, but the grace of God, which was with me." (1 Corinthians 15:10) You need to know that you must build off something. You cannot sit around and think that it will be given to you or that it will fall from the sky. It doesn't work that way. Start building by learning from your past failures and mistakes. If you fell in a ditch walking along a path and someone came along and pulled you out, would you fall into that hole again the next day? Surely, I would hope that you go around that hole and not fall in all over again. Life is about learning from our downfalls, our mistakes, and our failures.

You need to start setting time aside to study God's word. That is your food and the nourishment that you need for your body daily. You must eat the word of God in order to grow, and you must study the word of God to gain wisdom. You may have wisdom in this world, but you will never have the wisdom of Christ. The spirit has to teach you those things, and only those things will get you on your way to living and walking in Christ. You will begin waking up and thanking Jesus. You will desire to be closer to Him because this will be your protection, your guide, and your strength.

I just want to get you to the place of waiting only for God to make things happen for you. You may be sick and dying and the only way you can receive healing is believing and trusting in God. The doctors may have told you that you have days to live and there is nothing else that they can do on your behalf. Just stay in position, and God will truly come through.

You have to trust that. Your faith has to be operating and God has to show up on the scene. He will not allow you to look bad, and He won't let anyone other than Himself receive His credit. I encourage you to stay in position if you have been waiting on God and He still has not answered. I would patiently wait on God to prevail and make it happen. Anytime you trust God, you will wait on Him no matter what your situation looks like. You will wait because what you see is not what's real. However, what you cannot see is. The same is true with Jesus. We cannot see Him, but He's real. Likewise, when you give up on the promises of God, He sits at the right-hand throne and says, "Oh, ye of little faith."

Imagine yourself about to receive your blessings, and right when God is about to give you your gifts, you give up and get out of position. You have just missed out and now you have to start all over again just to receive the gift that was already yours from the beginning. I encourage you to just wait when you are going through. Any time you want to give up only means that your blessing is simply around the corner, and the enemy wants you to miss out.

He wants you to fail. He wants to see you give in, and he definitely wants to see you give out. If he can wait patiently for nothing, then surely you can wait on the promise. Our daddy owns this world. Do you not think that He will bless you? Surely, He will. He loves us just that much. All you have to do is ask, and it shall be given.

The enemy really gets busy when things start turning around for you and you start praising God in every aspect of your life. Let me give you an example of how he comes in unaware, tries to get you off the mark, and tries to make you lose focus. My husband was off on Wednesday night for the first time since he started attending Greater New Zion. We all headed out for church. However, when we got to church, I realized that there would be no service because we would be bringing the New Year in the very next day. So, we headed back to the house.

When we arrived, there was an unfamiliar car in our driveway. My husband got out to see who the driver was, and I hopped out behind him only to find out it was the repo guy. They came to take the car that I had gotten behind on with my monthly payments. I was hurt because I had gotten the vehicle for my mother when I brought her from Texas back to Louisiana to reside. I looked at her and the expression on her face let me knew that she was crushed as well. But God...

What seemed like a downfall was only a step up for us all. It was a debt that I could not afford any longer because I did not have a job anymore. It had been well over six months since I closed my office down. I told my mom not to worry and that God would provide. What seemed like it was bad was really a blessing in disguise. God really knows how to get things done. So, we cleaned out the car and gave the man the keys, and he drove off. I was hurt, disappointed, and broken behind a car that I could no longer afford.

I was more so hurt because it belonged to my mother. I thought that my whole world was crashing down on me. At least, that was the way I felt at the time. The funny part was when I brought it to God, He said that I already knew it was coming. He was right. It's not like it was unaware. I knew I had been avoiding the bill collectors. Consequently, they had to do what they had to do and pick the car up. I understood then and got over that situation quickly.

I want you to say, "Grow me up, God, so that I can operate in the gifts that you have given me. Teach me, Lord, so that I can build my faith daily. And, when a storm comes, I can stand." That was on a Wednesday night, and I was blessed with a job by Saturday. It was a job that all I had to do was show up and do little work for a lady named Grandmere. It was quiet at her residence, and it was only her and myself. I could study my bible and write my book without being distracted or interrupted by children.

This job was so easy that I worked every day for twelve hours and went home each morning feeling revived. I worked at nights and went home and prepared food for the day. (The kids and my husband would have a fit if I did not cook on a regular basis.) I was blessed with a simple job, and I used that time wisely. Meanwhile, I had been raising my niece, Alivia, for two years. Then, my time with her was up. I called her my niece because her mother and I were like sisters. Then, her mother came home from prison, and that relieved me from having to see her graduate from high school. God was really beginning to shine on me. I was beginning to see the evidence and His promises.

As the days passed and I was working nightly, God gave me a vision one morning while I was praying. It was a vision for my mother's car and how to go about getting it without having to pay anything down. I got excited because He showed me where to go and who to ask for. I was truly anxious and wanted to see this vision come to pass before my very eyes. I pulled up at the dealership, and I knew that my mother could not get another car because she had just gotten one a few months back for my daughter. So, there I was saying, "Okay, God. I trust you." I am telling you that you have to trust God with your whole heart, and then you have to wait patiently for Him to do His thing. He's good at all things.

My mother was not present, but God worked everything out. When God tell you to do something, you need to move quickly. If you do not, then you may just be missing out on your blessings. It's exciting when God gives you a right-now vision because you see His work right then and there. So I started the car-buying process and no one wanted to give her another car. She already had my daughter's car in her name, and the income just was not there. I called my dad on the phone and asked if I could have his suburban for a down payment. He agreed without question. I knew this was a God thing, because if you knew my dad, you knew the answer would have been no and the third degree. I was like, *okay God,* in the back of my mind. I was truly shocked.

The next day, I took my mother with me. I stopped at my dad's shop because he had to put a new battery in the truck. It had been sitting for over two years because the motor was going out, and the head gasket was blown completely.

My dad did not feel safe about me driving from Shreveport to Bossier in that truck. He and another mechanic told me that it simply wouldn't make it and that I would need to let them fix it. Without hesitation, I told them that I would take my chances. You may be thinking that I am foolish for not listening to these mechanics who know what they're talking about. However, when God tells you something, you better listen and not hear the words of man at all.

My dad then told me that he wanted to ride with me just in case the truck broke down. I declined his offer and told him that I would be fine because I already had a chauffeur, and Jesus was going to get me there safely. You have got to understand that I was operating off the vision that God had given me, and it was so plain. I drove that Suburban straight up Hearne Avenue and hopped on I-220 going to Bossier City with my mother and daughter behind me in the car that she was test driving.

I was floating the whole way. When I made it to the Benton Road exit and floated to the red light, I came to a complete stop. That is where the car died. You may be saying that I should have listened to the mechanics, but I need you to see the vision plain. I made it. I jumped out of the truck and got in with my mother. We drove on in to the dealership, and I told my sales rep that the truck stopped at the light. He went to the back and got three guys. In less than five minutes, the truck was on the lot. Furthermore, we still got a trade in value of $3055.00 for a 1999 GMC Suburban that was not fit for anyone. That is God.

On our way home, my mother said, "Girl your faith is so strong. I almost gave up but your faith never wavered." I told her that when God speaks a thing, it will surely come to pass. I told her that, I told you God gave me the vision plain. She then says to me, "He gave it to you and not me." I laughed and said, "Oh ye of little faith." I am so glad that is over. She got her car, and I was excited for being obedient and listening to the voice of the Lord. I am so glad about exercising my faith daily. You, too, must exercise your faith daily. Furthermore, you must learn to trust God. As a result, you will be able to stand when trials and tribulations come. That is how you will find strength when you need it.

You will quote God's word and believe what the word says about you. I shall live and not die. I am more than a conqueror through Him who loves me. I am the head and not the tail. I am above and not beneath. I can do all things through Christ that strengthens me. I will trust the Lord at all times. You will begin quoting the word and when you call those things out which be not, you shall have it.

When you go to your doctor's appointment and you are told that you have been diagnosed with cancer and only have six months to live, you will be able to stand on faith. For those of you that still have issues when it comes to trusting God, I want you to wake up every morning and say, "Lord, it is not easy, but I will trust you. Lord, I want you to help me with my unbelief and build me up where I am weak. Please order my steps and forgive me for my shortcomings in Jesus' name."

The Lord will set a standard up for you, and you will be able to rise against problems, sicknesses, strongholds, poverty, loneliness, worry, stress, and lack of faith. It is time to come out victorious because this battle isn't ours; it is the Lord's.

He is a rewarder to those who diligently seek Him. I want you to start leaning to God and not your own understanding. I want you to look to the hills from which comes your help. All of it comes from the Lord. Faith is the only thing that moves God. So, without it it's impossible to please Him. He gave each of us a measure of faith. We just have to grow it. It's like a dollar bill. I can spend it and have nothing, or I can invest it and let it grow. Which will you choose?

Chapter Four

Greater is Coming

In this season, God is really doing a new thing. One Sunday, I got to church only to find out that my pastor was not there, and we had a visiting pastor named Overseer Whitaker. When I tell you that he brought a word. OMG… It was good. He talked about the process and the promise. He talked about people focusing on the palace and forgetting about the pit. It is the pit that gets you to the palace. He went on to say that we do not want to praise and thank God when we're in the pit. We only want to praise and worship God in the palace. In the process, we complain, fuss, get upset, and give up. Yet, being in the process is the only thing that is going to make us stronger for what is ahead. So, stop griping about being in the pit and allow God to work on you so that you can get to the palace.

I had a doctor's appointment for them to check my blood and to give me Zometa to strengthen my bones from the chemo and to build my calcium back up. I did not need it, but I would go so that I could see all the cancer patients. I enjoy telling them about Jesus. When I got there this day, I was talking to a lady about what stage she was in and how it had spread all over her body. She told me she was a stage two when she came and was currently a stage four.

She talked to me in hopes that Jesus would keep her for her kids. I told her that she must believe and that God would do it. I asked her if she believed and she said she did. I told her that I would pray for her before she left if she wanted me to do so. I suppose you know what took place; I prayed as I laid hands on her. When I finished praying for her, another lady that was present asked if I would pray for her, too. Of course, I allowed God to use me in the spirit.

      I prayed for those women that day. Now, each time I go to the Feist Weiler clinic, I testify, pray, and lay hands on those people. I even pray for the nurses and give them word from on high. God is truly using me in this season. *I will go, Lord. Send me. Take me higher, oh God, and teach me your ways, your statutes, your judgements, and your commandments.* Psalm 23 says, "The Lord is my shepherd, I shall not want. He makes me to lie down in green pastures: He leads me beside the still waters. He restores my soul: He leads me in the path of righteousness for his name's sake. Yea, though I walk through the valley of the shadow of death, I will fear no evil: for thou art with me; thy rod and thy staff they comfort me. Thou prepare a table before me in the presence of mine enemies: thou anoint my head with oil; my cup runs over. Surely goodness and mercy shall follow me all the days of my life: and I will dwell in the house of the Lord forever."

      I want you to start preparing your hearts and minds for Jesus so that you will be able to operate fully and hear God's voice clearly. I pray that as you continue reading this book, you will begin to clean up your house. There is no room for dust. That means that if it is not God's business, then I have no time for foolishness. I need to get everything that God has for me. Therefore, the things that I thought were right, I am now letting go and looking to Him to guide me. I want you to look back at your past and anything that you want to hide under the rug. Now, confess and confront that thing. That is the stronghold that is keeping you from deliverance. That is the thing that is keeping you from the promises of God.

Many are called, but few are chosen. The first way you can look at this scenario is you were called but went astray. You know that God had a calling on your life, yet you refused to accept the calling. Then, the chosen ones are the ones that are called and accept it. They embrace their calling and start seeking the will of God. They desire to be like David and be after God's own heart. These are the people who love the Lord their God with all their heart, mind, and soul.

Life's experiences can be summed up as the process of trial and error. We all make choices. Sometimes, those choices may have heavy consequences attached to them. All too often, when one makes a poor choice, the result is that poor choice being highlighted, which usually overshadows any good deed. You are shunned by society with a negative stigma permanently attached, and every right step you attempt to make is accompanied by your past faults constantly being thrown in your face. Again, my past failures built my faith. As a believer of God and faith, you live and you learn from them.

Focus on your potentials and not your limitations. Dr. Martin Luther King said, "The ultimate measure of a man is not where he stands in moments of comfort and convenience, but where he stands at times of challenge and controversy." Joshua 1:9 says, "be strong and of good courage; be not afraid, neither be thou dismayed: for the Lord thy God is with thee whithersoever thou goest." I want you to start resting in Jesus. The bible says in

Matthew 11:28, "Come unto me all ye that labor and are heavy and I will give you rest." Start affirming daily: I am resting in the arms of the Eternal. In God's peace, I find rest for the body, the mind, and the soul. The everlasting healing presence of the eternal steals away my tension and my thoughts. For the stress of each new day, the peace that surpasses understanding is mine in depth. I rest in the Lord and wait patiently for Him.

Chapter Five

A Wounded Mother

The enemy comes to steal, kill, and destroy, and he was really trying to take me out. However, he no longer had me bound, so he started attacking the ones I love the most. If you know me, you know not to mess with my children or my money. I will do you something drastic to protect them. My son got shot late one night. When the phone call came, it did not scare me at all. I was already mentally prepared for that. I knew that my son would either end up in prison or six feet under the ground. Jail or death was lurking around my front door. I had just gotten him out on bail about a month prior to the night he got shot. He was out on bail for three armed robberies.

When he got to the house, I tried to tell him that he needed to slow down and start thinking. That was his problem, he never thought about the consequences until it was over and ended badly. I knew he got that from me because I was a menace in every way. Nothing or no one was going to stop me from working for the devil.

As time went on, I got hit repeatedly with another jab to my heart. My son went back to jail on a murder charge. Yet, I was a praying mother that was interceding for him. There had to be justice in that situation. If you did not do the crime, it was hard to do the time. Nevertheless, I got to prove his innocence. I was so grateful that my mom had moved back to Shreveport from Dallas after twenty plus years, and she became my strength to fight all these battles. We faced them together. We paid for an attorney and a private investigator because we needed justice. In addition, we started praying that God would prevail and set him free. We asked God to please show Himself mighty and to pull down strongholds.

Now, don't you dare think that I had any money to just give to these people. I had to go to the casino and play as if I was rich and loaded with money. After a night of gambling, I walked out of Margaritaville early one morning with over six grand for the private investigator. I went in with three-hundred dollars and worked it like I had thousands. I know some of you may be wondering why didn't I activate my faith so that God could move on my behalf. Well, I did; it just was not in the right way. No matter how you look at it, I was still operating in faith.

While dealing with my son and the justice system, another storm approached. My husband-to-be had to go before eternal affairs to see if he would be able to keep his job. He's a police officer, and he truly serves and protects. If you knew him personally, you would know that he's a very humble and honest human being. You would probably even ask how in the world we hooked up. It's because when God joins something together, no man can tear it apart. Waiting on God was the best thing I could have ever done.

While dealing with my son's and my husband-to-be's storms, I was hit with a storm of my own and charged with accessory after the fact to murder. As you can see, the enemy was definitely trying to take me out. However, I continued to keep my head held high. But again, there was another blow to my heart. I was no longer working for myself because they were trying to build a case as if I was practicing law without a license. So, I closed my office. After that, I was charged again with forgery. They did not even have a case number or a complainant. Still, they were throwing that storm my way to add to the other storms. If that was not enough, I got diagnosed with Stage IV breast cancer amid it all. The devil was really trying to prevent me from being about my Father's business.

When God tells you something, do not allow man to trip you up to think that your faith isn't activated. All that the enemy has thrown your way is working together for your good. "For I know the thoughts that I think toward you, says the Lord, thoughts of peace, and not of evil, to give you an expected end." (Jeremiah 29:11) Although life may throw curveballs here and there, you still have to love your enemies. Bless them that curse you, do good to them that hate you, and pray for them which despitefully use you; that you may be the children of your Father which is in heaven. As we consider those who harm us, we are wise to remember our former status as enemies of God. But God reconciled us to Himself through Christ and gave us the ministry of reconciliation. Now, we have a holy obligation. He has committed to us the message of reconciliation. We as Christians are to take that message to the world and refrain from getting discouraged when the message is not received by everyone.

You have to realize that when Jesus walked the earth and performed miracles, those people did not believe and had little to almost no faith at all. If He was not widely received, we shouldn't expect the road to be much smoother for us. We are His children, and we should be putting our faith to work daily and allowing it to grow. That way when circumstances and storms come our way, we will be able to stand until we come out victorious. For, this battle isn't ours, but the Lord's. He has already paid the price, and our problems are only light afflictions to Him.

Take a moment and think about the goodness of God. I want you to meditate on one thing that God has brought you out of, and I want you to really think about how you thought that you wouldn't survive it. Think about how you thought it was over for you, how you could not see the light of day, and how no one knew the pain you felt. Now, say, "But God." Oh, how our daddy loves us so! He paid a debt that He did not owe all because He loves us just that much. We should be denying ourselves daily and picking up our cross to follow Jesus. We should be running to spread the good news of the Lord.

Chapter Six

The Impact

I remember going to Atlanta, Georgia one year when I was just a kid. As we passed a local church, I read a message that impacted my heart and stuck with me from then to now. It was so plain and vividly written: "Dusty bibles lead to dirty lives." I thought about my bible, and I just knew that the saying was written just for me. I did not have to go home and look at my bible to know if it had accumulated dust. I knew that it had, and I wanted to do something about it. I encourage you to keep the dust off your bibles. You have to make each moment your best, and count it all joy when you fall into temptation. You must clean up daily by reading the word and living your life according to it. You cannot just talk the talk and not walk the walk. There are people watching you, and you should be setting the example of Christ for them to follow.

We never know the impact we place on someone's life until they share it in a message on how they overcame or became bound by what you lived. I read a poem once by Edgar A. Guest entitled "Sermons We See." It reads:

"SERMONS WE SEE"

I'd rather see a sermon than hear one any day.
I'd rather one should walk with me than merely show the way.
The eye's a better pupil and more willing than the ear;
Fine counsel is confusing, but example's always clear;

And the best of all the preachers are the men who live their creeds,
For to see the good in action is what everybody needs.
I can soon learn how to do it if you'll let me see it done.
I can watch your hands in action, but your tongue too fast may run.
And the lectures you deliver may be very wise and true;
But I'd rather get my lesson by observing what you do.
For I may misunderstand you and the high advice you give,
But there's no misunderstanding how you act and how you live.

People are watching even the smallest gestures. We may unknowingly be someone's up as well as someone's down. That is why we should give and do our best always. We never know who is watching and how we impact others by the way we live.

    I remember having good and bad teachers. I also remember having caring and uncaring teachers, as well as the ones that impacted my life. It was not hard to pick the good apples from the bad ones. And, we all know what to do with bad apples in our lives. We have to throw them away rather than cut off the rotten parts and keep them. Just throw them out. You know the saying, "One bad apple will spoil the whole bunch." I agree with it wholeheartedly.

    I remember having a math teacher at Midway Middle School named Mr. Levy. He was such an inspiring teacher. He was truly born to teach math, and he taught it well. He was so good that even the slower learners learned from him. He had the patience of Rebekah in the bible, and no room for foolishness. When you walked into his classroom, you were coming in to learn and that was it. He was a stern teacher who meant business and no play. He would tell us that we would thank and appreciate him later in life. He was so right, and he was one that impacted my life for the good.

I also remember having a teacher in the same school just doors down from Mr. Levy named Mrs. Thomas. She was a science teacher, and I have the slightest clue on how she graduated. You would have thought that she was our age. Her maturity level was of a kid, and all she did was make jokes and curse. You did not have to work in her class if she liked you. When we did work, we just read straight from the text. I happened to be one of the students she liked, which meant I did no work.

I would leave the school grounds with her permission to walk to John's Seafood to get something to eat. She would be okay with that just as long as I brought her a meal back. The seafood place was not next door either. It was about eight blocks from the school. So, you see how much she cared. There was no work and all play when students entered her classroom. We thought that Mrs. Thomas was cool and a great teacher. However, little did we know, she was truly hurting us. We would suffer in the long run. That was the negative impact on my life.

Going down memory lane, I remember Coach Snow being the detention teacher for students who got disciplined for misconduct or misbehavior at school. Those students had to go to his class for in-school suspension. He was mean and did not play with any kids. Detention students had to write lines and keep quiet. If they did not, he had a paddle that he believed in using without your parent's permission. Now, what I admire about him was the fact that he would always talk to the kids and try to come to a solution for their behavior. He was such a problem solver when it came to kids that misbehaved. He just had that gift to deal with behavioral kids.

I was one of those kids that went to his class often. I was not a bad kid, and my grades were always good. In fact, I would get finished with my work in class, and then I would say or do something stupid just to go to his class. I liked going to hear him point out a kid's problem and then find a resolution for that problem. He soon discovered my reason for coming to his class, and he solved my problem as well. I became his assistant, and I could go to his class after I finished my work in other classes to help with assisting all the other kids. He taught me to be a problem solver, and that was the impact in my life for the good.

All of these life experiences have taught me to be who I am. They taught me that we cannot dictate life based on what happened in our past. We cannot allow those things to keep us bound. Let those things build character and faith in God. You are somebody, and the enemy uses past failures to keep you in bondage in hopes that you will never receive the light in a dark tunnel. He wants to keep you blinded, and as long as he does, he is winning. We must rise to the occasion to get the necessary tools to fight daily.

You have to sometimes encourage yourself in the Lord your God. You must step out on faith and wait patiently on the promises. Stay steadfast and unmovable always abounding the work of the Lord, and wait upon the Lord. Acknowledge that you are nothing without God and you are everything with Him. "But, by the grace of God, I am what I am: and His grace which was bestowed upon me was not in vain; but I labored more abundantly than they all: yet not I but the grace of God which was with me." (1 Corinthians 15:10)

Everyone has to get a scripture on the inside of them so when the enemy comes, you will have word to stand on. You need to find the scripture that moves you, keeps you, and allows you to tap into your inner spirit or also known as the God in you. That spirit knows how to build faith and utter words that we cannot describe.

Chapter Seven

The Walls of Jericho

We all have walls and not all of them are built on what God has purposed for our lives. I found myself fasting on a Tuesday during our corporate fast at church. I cannot recall ever joining in on this fast; and, if I did it was so long ago that I cannot remember. That is sad, but it is true. I have always made excuses when it came to fasting. However, this Tuesday God, spoke to my spirit and ordered me to fast that day. I believe that when we sacrifice with fasting and praying, God does things to broaden our spiritual being and equip us to tap into a higher arena. During this fast, I found myself studying the word to remain spiritually fed. Otherwise, I would have definitely become hungry in the natural. The flesh will give in if you do not stay focused in the word.

As I was meditating and studying the word, I was led by God to start a Jericho walk the very next day. God spoke to me and led me to pick up the phone to call Evangelist Barbara which is my oldest daughter's God mother. I told her that I wanted to come over and pray. Then, I asked her to call her friend, Sister Pat, and tell her to come over as well. When I arrived, they were both waiting for me, and we wasted no time to start prayer. As we prayed, the spirit of the Lord filled the atmosphere.

It was mind blowing because on that day, I was renewed fully operating in the gift that I received in 2004. I was so happy that God had allowed me another chance to do His work. I am always saying that I trust God. However, that day, God was saying to me, "I trust you." Now, that is an awesome feeling! You would have to experience it to know the high that I was on that day.

Afterwards, I was led to tell them about the Jericho walk the very next day and that I would start at six o'clock in the morning. Everyone was excited and wanted God to move on our behalf. It would definitely be a sacrifice for myself, and I was ready to do what God had instructed me to do. It was really dark the next morning, and we needed a safe place to walk. The Spirit led us to go to Lowes because they have a pretty large parking lot, lots of lights, and the employees are there before 6:00 a.m. Nevertheless, this was the perfect place.

Sister Pat and I showed up at the same time. The spirit of the Lord directed me by saying that we will walk and speak Psalm 23. "The Lord is my shepherd; I shall not want. He makes me to lie down in green pastures: He leads me beside the still waters. He restores my soul: He leads me in the paths of righteousness for his name's sake. Yea, though I walk through the valley of the shadow of death, I will fear no evil: for thou art with me; thy rod and thy staff they comfort me. Thou prepares a table before me in the presence of mine enemies: thou anoint my head with oil; my cup runs over. Surely goodness and mercy shall follow me all the days of my life: and I will dwell in the house of the Lord forever." It also happened to be twenty-third day of the month, and we both knew that scripture.

Day one was awesome and the Spirit of the Lord was truly moving. Evangelist Barbara did not make it because she had to be to work for 5:00 a.m. On day two, we all were present, and God gave me Joshua 24:1-16.

Verse 15 says, "And if it seems evil unto you to serve the Lord, choose you this day whom ye will serve, whether the gods which your fathers served that were on the other side of the flood, or the gods of the Amorites, in whose land ye dwell: but as for me and my house, we will serve the Lord."

On day three, we all were present again, and we began our walk around that city tearing down walls that were built. God gave me Lamentations 3:22-25 which says, "It is of the Lord's mercies that we are not consumed, because his compassions fail not. They are new every morning: great is thy faithfulness. The Lord is my portion, saith my soul; therefore, will I hope in him. The Lord is good unto them that wait for him, to the soul that seeketh Him."

Day four, I awoke early and God had given me word. However, He told me that word was for me alone, so I wrestled with not having a word to give to them that morning. I got to them and told them that I did not have a scripture because God had not given me one. God then spoke to me and said that today would be praise and worship. He said that our praise and worship would shift the atmosphere. God was truly moving, and all I desired was to be in His presence. I was definitely chasing after Him.

Day five, I woke up and headed to Lowes. This day it rained and the devil did not want us being faithful. Despite the slight rain, we still walked. The walls were being torn down, and I could sense the move of God. He was present in every way. That morning, He gave me Psalm 27, "The Lord is my light and my salvation; whom shall I fear? The Lord is the strength of my life; of whom shall I be afraid?

"When the wicked, even mine enemies and my foes, came upon me to eat up my flesh, they stumbled and fell. Though a host should encamp against me, my heart shall rise against me, in this will I be confident. One thing have I desired of the Lord, that will I seek after; that I may dwell in the house of the Lord all the days of my life, to behold the beauty of the Lord, and to inquire in his temple. For in the time of trouble he shall hide me in his pavilion: in the secret of his tabernacle shall he hide me; he shall set me upon a rock.

"And now shall mine head be lifted up above mine enemies round about me: therefore will I offer in his tabernacle sacrifices of joy; I will sing, yea, I will sing praises unto the Lord. Hear, O Lord, when I cry with my voice: have mercy also upon me, and answer me. When thou saidst, Seek ye my face; my heart said unto thee, Thy face, Lord, will I seek. Hide not thy face far from me; put not thy servant away in anger: thou hast been my help; leave me not, neither forsake me, O God of my salvation. When my father and my mother forsake me, then the Lord will take me up.

"Teach me thy way, O Lord and lead me in a plain path, because of mine enemies. Deliver me not over unto the will of mine enemies: for false witnesses are risen up against me, and such as breathe out cruelty. I had fainted, unless I had believed to see the goodness of the Lord in the land of the living. Wait on the Lord: be of good courage, and he shall strengthen thine heart: wait, I say, on the Lord."

It was a reason that David said wait on the Lord twice. He wanted you to understand what it is to wait and have patience in waiting on the Lord. If we fail to wait and go along as if we were never waiting, or perhaps we get tired of waiting, we risk missing out on what God has for us. Our blessing is just around the corner, yet our impatience tells God not to worry about the gift that He was about to bless us with. God wants to bless you, but if you are not willing to wait upon the Lord, then you will find yourself missing out big time. I encourage you today to wait on the Lord.

Day six, we did worship and prayer. I began petitioning and making my requests known to God. I was believing that He was about to do a new thing. From the day I started that walk, my life had never been the same. As our walk was coming to an end, we had been faithful in getting up each morning, and we were counting on God to move on our behalf. We walked each day with expectancy, and I was going to stand until I saw the manifestation of all that we were desiring from God. John 14:14 says, "Whatever I ask in Jesus' name, He will do it."

On the last day, we began our walk. It was really cold that morning, and we had to walk seven times around the city. We were walking in the promises of God. So, we walked and praised the name of the Lord. That morning, He gave me revelation by saying to me, "All you need is grace. I can cover a multitude." For me, that was mind-blowing because it is His grace that covers me, keeps me, and loves me just for me. The same love that He has for me is the same love He has for you. He is the reason there is no cure for cancer and the reason I am cancer free today.

I encourage each of you to tap into the promises of God. I can do all things through Christ that strengthens me. It is such an awesome feeling when you have the power to heal, get wealth, lay hands, move situations, operate in His anointing, and make demons flee. That is such an awesome feeling of knowing that you possess the same spiritual anointing that Jesus possessed when He walked this earth.

We used to sing a song that said, "Yes, Jesus loves me. Yes, Jesus loves me. For the bible tells me so." I think that we personally need to go back to that so we can be reminded of God's love for us. "He has the whole world in His hand. He has the whole wide world in His hand" is another song that we must not forget. That is a reminder that our daddy owns everything. Therefore, we should not fret over light afflictions and small matters. The key is we have to start operating in right now faith. I stress this because it is urgent, vital, and so important.

I want you to have a fresh anointing by the time you finish this book. I want you to get it in your spirit that you believe and that you trust God no matter what. The Hebrew boys said in the fire that they knew that their God was able to save them. Then, they said, if He does not, it is not because He can't. We serve a God that is going to show up on our behalf just like He did for them and for Elijah when he stood before those four-hundred fifty false prophets. God showed up for the Hebrew boys and Elijah, and the people had to bow down and worship our God.

Our daddy will not let us down. He will never

leave us nor forsake us. He will stick closer than a brother. He is your strength, and I want you to know this. I dare you to start trusting and relying on God today. Your life will never be the same.

Chapter Eight

It Works

I know that you have tried a few things in life, and they did not work. Perhaps you have tried lots of things, and they just did not seem to work in your favor. You may feel that you just do not want to try anything else. Sometimes we feel like the jinx is on us and that everything we do or touch fails. You may feel like the third wheel, the black sheep, the lone ranger, or even like enough is enough. If you have failed in all these things, it is because you have not tried God.

See, I believe that when you try God, you cannot fail. You deny yourself and allow God to operate, lead, and guide you every step of the way. He knows what is best, and He has our best interest at heart. He wants nothing but greater for us and he will give us the desires of our heart just as long as we line up with the word. He wants to bless us and enlarge our territory. Try Him, and watch Him work.

Appointment

I headed north to Hearne Ave because I had an appointment with a lady named Ronda at Good Life. I set this appointment because I wanted to know what natural herbs I should take to keep myself healthy. When I arrived, I let the cashier know that I had a 1:30 appointment. A guy escorted me to the back, and I sat down to wait for her. I was a little early and she was eating, so it was about fifteen minutes before she came and got me.

I stepped inside her office. Immediately, she tested my eyes and told me everything that was wrong with me. She was really good at her work. She told me that I was a very strong person, and that I could take a lot. She told me about my lower left back - the side that I call my thorn in my flesh - and she told me about my right breast. This lady was really on it and everything was on point.

Be reminded that I am healed. I just wanted to stay healthy by eating right and keeping my body up. I wanted to take whatever natural herbs would keep me from becoming sick all over again. It is said that the eyes are the window into your soul. Jesus spoke about this when He taught on how our eyes reflect either spiritual light or great spiritual darkness within our souls. "The light of the body is the eye: if therefore thine eye be single, the whole body shall be full of light. But if thine eye be evil, thy whole body shall be full of darkness. If therefore the light that is in thee be darkness, how great is that darkness." (Matthew 6:22-23) In this verse, Jesus makes certain that there is no misunderstanding that either we are full of light, or we are in great darkness. Just as we cannot love two masters, so that there cannot be any neutrality in the state of our souls.

What makes the difference between an eye full of light and an eye full of darkness? To know this, you have to understand light and know where darkness comes from. Spiritual darkness came upon all mankind without exception in the Garden of Eden when Adam and Eve rebelled against God. Adam and Eve's pride drove them to eat of the tree of knowledge of good and evil. Because of that, "when they knew God, they glorified Him not as God, neither were thankful; but became vain in their imaginations, and their foolish heart was darkened." (Romans 1:21)

The Spirit is the light that rekindles the light that was darkened by our sin of Adam. Through the Spirit is presence and power. Each person in whom the Spirit dwells becomes the light of the world. Matthew 5:14 says, "You are the light of the world. A city that is set on a hill that cannot be hid, so I encourage you to let your light so shine before men, that they may see your good works, and glorify your Father which is in heaven." (Matthew 5:16) So it is true when they say that the eyes are the window into your soul.

Chapter Nine

Faith for Finances

Our intercessors from Greater New Zion went to Michigan for a prayer conference. It was mind-blowing the three days we were there. On our way there, Mrs. Kim was escorted by wheelchair because she had been going through some serious health issues since 2012 and almost missed the opportunity of getting healed. So she pressed her way to go, and while being there, she received her healing. On our way back from Michigan, she was not only walking alongside with us, but she was pulling luggage as well. Tell me what our God cannot and will not do! I believe that she had to get like the lady with the issue of blood. If she could just touch the hem of His garment, she knew she would be healed. Mrs. Kim's faith moved God for her healing. It was an awesome and radical experience that I will never forget. I believe that everyone was healed, delivered, and set free from something.

I also had such an awesome roommate named Tina. We clicked quickly, and the rest was history. I woke up the next morning, and she was already awake stirring around preparing to attend service. I asked her if she saw my bald head, which I know she did, and I asked if she would pray over me. I wanted her to lay hands on my head and believe God with me to grow my hair back speedily. You may be saying that I should be thankful for the healing and not worried about my hair growing back. However, I'm here to tell you that God will give you the desires of your heart as well. So, backup and allow me to receive what God is about to do for me and that is grow my hair back.

We got dressed and went to service with our minds ready to receive what God had for us. The first day, God told me that I would possess and over take the land - a land flowing with milk and honey. I was truly excited because I was thinking that God was going to send me to someone to claim and possess a land. Yet, I did not know this until day two. On that day, I took a class called Faith for Finances. I learned that it is not about the finances, but it is your faith that will get you the finances that you need. This was awesome because I have now stepped into a new arena. I understand now what I once did not or could not quite seem to grasp. I was about to blow up. Boom! I knew that God was about to take me higher than I had ever been or ever could imagine. I am truly grateful because God has given me an extension on my life. I shall live and not die.

That night in service, I received revelation from God that if I could put a demand on Him, surely I could put a demand on the people. I was thinking, *Oh so you mean to tell me that I will not get this land freely*. God told me, "I said that you will possess and overtake the land that is filled with milk and honey." He told me that I would ask for one-hundred thousand dollars from the church and that my family would start with two thousand. The first thing I told God was "You know that I do not have the funds, and that I am trying to get out of debt." He then said to me that I would sow where I want to go.

I want you to understand this revelation. When God tells you to do something, do it and do not procrastinate or sit on a vision or a command that God has given you. I want you to trust Him. If it takes you to start taking baby steps, then do that. Still, learn to trust God no matter what your situation looks like, no matter what it feels like. Just trust Him.

Some people may look at my cancer as a curse, while others may look at it as being sad. I think neither and that cancer was a blessing for me. Yes, you read that correctly. Cancer was truly my blessing, and God knows just what we need to get back on track. I am now forever grateful, and what the enemy meant for my bad, God turned it around for my good. He could have stopped the enemy from attacking me, but He knew that it would work for my good. Hence, so He allowed me to go through it. He also allowed me to get closer to Him and develop a stronger relationship with Him. Each morning I am renewed, and I look to the hills which comes my help. All my help comes from the Lord.

The prayer conference was going well. On day three, God simply told me to just move. He did not say anything else. Just move. This was our last night in Michigan, and we were all sitting around telling our testimonies and how God had delivered us from so many strongholds. We had so many testimonies until it kept us up all night. We did not have the opportunity of going to bed, and that was okay because we enjoyed the sisterhood of getting to know each other.

Despite our past failures, we all had something in common - we were on the rise. We were all God-chasers, and we were all shifting in this season. We were all filled with a renewed spirit as we headed for the airport. We were the army that is rising to the occasion. That experience was one that will forever be a life changing experience and not for just the intercessors who attended the conference, but for Greater New Zion as well.

Sunday came, and I was placed on protocol. Likewise, I put a demand on the people just as God gave it to me. It was such an awesome Sunday because it was much different. The church was filled and God moved in that place. The message came from Isaiah 40:31, "But they that wait upon the Lord shall renew their strength; they shall mount up with wings as eagles; they shall run, and not be weary; and they shall walk, and not faint."

Bishop said that we were about to fly. He said that when we do fly, we should not worry about flying or soaring high because when we land, we would have a perfect landing. I believe I can fly. Do you believe that you can fly? I believe I can touch the sky. Do you believe that you can touch the sky? I ask this because you cannot go off my faith for your situation. You will need your own faith to operate and to move God. I have my faith, and it works. Build your own faith.

Chapter Ten

I Was Doing it BIG

The devil had me thinking that I was doing it big. There I was, a twenty-year-old female who had mad hustle in me. I was off the chain. I had the city sown up, and I was well-respected by those who lived the lifestyle that I lived because I got mine. Furthermore, everyone knew that I was straight business, and playing games and befriending people was not in the equation. I had very few people in my circle. You would have considered me to be that ride or die female, and you most definitely wanted me on your team. By the time I turned twenty-three, I had a new hustle. I was traveling from state to state and doing it big. I was hitting three banks a day for nine thousand, seven hundred, and eighty-eight dollars or more. I just had to make sure I did not go over that ten-thousand-dollar mark for them to report it to the IRS.

I was rolling, and I was on a different flight every week going to a different state. I was truly living the life and thought that it was good. Little did I know, I was going straight to hell. I remember getting off the plane and checking into the Hyatt Hotel. I called a company who had bodyguards and hired a crew for the day. I rode around Miami as if I was a celeb and people were trying to figure out who I was and what I did for a living. All they knew in their mind was I was someone big. I went shopping, and my bodyguards were right there surrounding me.

As I entered Neiman's, the sales representative flocked to me as if I was worth millions. I was truly getting a kick out of all this attention. When I checked out they never asked for identification for the stuff I purchased. I had Jimmy Choo, Prada, Louis Vuitton, Gucci, Marc Jacobs, and Burberry. I had sunglasses, dresses, purses, and shoes. I had it all, and this was not my money by far nor was it my credit cards. My bodyguards would grab my bags, and we would leave the stores.

I was so tickled on the inside because this was a hustle that only a savage could devise. I am telling you that looks are truly deceiving. I got dropped back off at the hotel and requested to be picked up later that night for the club. I was about to do it big, and I was going to shine. It was a quarter past eleven when I got picked up. I had on a black BCBG dress that hugged me in all the right places, and a pair of Jimmy Choo stilettos. My hair was hanging long, and my highlights gave me that extra glamour look. I wore no foundation, but I had on eyeliner, mascara, and lip gloss to enhance my beauty. I truly looked good, and I was ready for the night to set prey for the next baller who thought that I was somebody big.

The bodyguard knocked at the room door, and I grabbed my purse as I opened the door to exit. We got on the elevator, and he pressed the lobby floor. We got off the elevator and headed towards the limousine. As I was stepping in my four-inch stilettos, the bodyguard could not resist telling me that I looked stunning. He said, "I do not mean to be disrespectful, but I will not pass the opportunity of telling you how good you look." I said thanks in a way that let him knew I was used to the compliments. He opened the car door for me, and I stepped inside the limo. I sat back and envisioned my next move. I was headed to the scene to see what duck I could pluck. I was all about the Benjamins, and I was about to get over on somebody.

We arrived at the Player's Choice club and one of the bodyguards let me out. I make my way to the door with both body guards side by side. All eyes were on me as the people wondered who I was. I was dying laughing on the inside. I got inside and went straight to VIP. I do not drink alcohol, so I ordered a coke and told them to put it in a champagne glass just for the look. As I sipped the coke, I scanned the room unnoticeably. I had my eyes on the money. He was staring at me, and if eyes could undress someone, I was naked. He strolled over and my bodyguards stood in front of him. He leaned over to tell me to let my boys know that we were friends and it was okay for him to enter.

I laughed and told them it was okay, and he approached me. Then, he asked if I was expecting someone. I tell him no and that I was just there to unravel my feathers. He laughed and asked if he could sit. I pointed at the seat, and he obeyed and sat down opposite of me. He told me that his name was Roe and that he played for the Miami Dolphins. In my mind, I said, "*Bingo. I got a jackpot.*" I knew he was trying to impress me because he wanted me to know exactly who he was and that his money was long. It was good for me, because he did not ask my status nor who I was. He just thought he had a celeb. That was how I rolled, and that was the way I was coming.

We talked for a long time, and I got to know all I needed to know about him. This mouse was married, and I was the cat that was about to eat him alive. He wanted something, and so did I. I was listening to all this blah, blah, blah about him and the wifey not on good terms and that he was planning a way to escape without having to pay alimony on top of child support. *Yeah, yeah, yeah,* I thought. *This fool thinks I'm slow and naïve.* Nevertheless, I was loving it.

So, there I was telling him about my next business plan and how I work with sponsors to donate to battered children. I also told him that I helped with the Christmas drive, Thanksgiving, and other programs helping children. He immediately said that I could count him in for one-hundred thousand for the first year, and depending on how nice I was, he would be donating more each year.

I felt secure in that matter. I told him that I was exhausted because I had business the next day and that we could link up afterwards. I told him that I would be in town for a few weeks depending on how this conference meeting went and if all the sponsors signed contracts. He asked if he could participate and sign his contract as well. I told him that was cool and that I had to draft up the contract. I got up and his mouth dropped as he reached to whisper in my ear.

He said, "I really like you, and I really want more of you. I will take care of you, and you won't be disappointed. I believe in taking care of my woman, and a woman like you deserves for a man to lavish her with nice gifts that she does not have to go out and buy on her own. Just give me this time that you are here, and I will let you decide afterwards."

I said okay as I beckoned for my bodyguards. He grabbed my phone and dialed his number. He told me that he would be calling me, but requested that I call him as soon I made it back to the hotel. I nodded in agreeance, and then we parted ways. I went out the door, and he headed towards the men's room. I wanted to jump up and down because I had no idea how this trip would turn out, but I came expecting to receive.

  To make money, you have to have money was one of my sayings. There I was in Miami living it up as if I was rich and had it. That was a bad girl, but she had faith in doing whatever she desired. If I thought it, it came to pass. If I wanted something, I got it. I did not realize these were spiritual gifts that I was using in the wrong way. I just thought that I had the gift of gab. I thought that I was just that smooth. I had no idea that the gifts God gives are without repentance. I just knew I could make people do what I wanted.

  I arrived back at the hotel and tipped my driver along with my bodyguards. I gave them all a grand a piece and that did not include my services. It was my way of tipping. Everyone deserves a tip when they do well, and they did well. They had no idea I was not the female they thought I was. I let them know that I would call them when I was ready to be picked up and that I would be okay going back upstairs alone.

  I headed to the elevators and when I stepped into the room. I took my stilettos off and dived straight for the bed. I was jumping up and down and could not stop my excitement because I had just made myself one-hundred-thousand dollars, and all I spent out was about five grand. This was definitely an investment. I calmed myself as I walked to the bathroom. I looked in the mirror and said to myself, "You are one bad mother." Then, I dialed the number to reach Roe. He answered as if he was waiting anxiously by the phone. I said hello and then I went on to say that I really enjoyed him and that I would see him the next day because I was tired. That was my way of letting him know that he could not stop by my room.

I relaxed by playing some music on my laptop. Then, I ran myself some bubble bath and lit a candle. I undressed to get in the tub and tried relaxing, but I was too tickled because of my accomplishment. I could stay for a week without hustling. I was about to see what lavish meant in the eyes of Roe. The next morning, I woke up to see that he had called three times and left a message. He was saying that he was ready to spend some time with me. I called him up as if I had been in conferences all morning. He said he understood but was making sure I did not bounce on him and go home. I laughed as if to say "not without my check. I told him that I would be finished around noon and that he was more than welcome to come and pick me up. We both agreed that I would be waiting downstairs for his arrival.

I hung the phone up and called the limousine company for them to arrive at eleven because I was ready for service. The bodyguards showed up just as I finished glossing in the bathroom. That day, I wore a black Ralph Lauren skirt suit with a fly red dress shirt underneath and red Prada heels to compliment. I had my Prada purse on my shoulder as I opened the door and greeted my bodyguards. I told them that I would only need them for an hour or so, and they would be free to go for the day.

I was lounging on the couch when Roe walked in with a single rose in hand. He approached me and bent to kiss me on the cheek. Then, he handed me the rose. I said, "Thank you." That is when he asked if I went anywhere without bodyguards. I told him I did but not often. He asked if I could relieve them because he wanted to take me out on the town.

    I walked over to the bodyguards and told them that I would take care of them the next day. They agreed, and I walked back over to Roe. He grabbed me by the hand, and we walked towards the door. I was astonished with his expensive taste. He was driving a black Bentley with cream interior and the seats were soft leather. I was definitely in for a treat. We headed uptown, and he bought me a red Marc Valvo dress that cost over two grand. He also bought me a Gucci bag with the matching wallet and heels. He bought perfume and paid over a grand for a necklace and earrings that looked like they came from Claire's. He even tried buying me Gucci luggage. I declined because I had Louis Vuitton luggage and did not want any more luggage to carry back on the plane with me.

    We went to a fine five-star restaurant, and I ordered lobster and scampi shrimp, salad, and a glass of water. He was pleased to know that I did not drink either and said that he was looking forward to getting to know more about this mystery young woman with bodyguards. I laughed, and we carried on with conversation. At the end of the day, we walked the beach. I rocked a turquoise two-piece bathing suit that looked great on me and revealing all my tattoos. We strolled the beach holding hands and talking nonstop. He asked the question if I enjoyed flying? I told him that I was a bird that had to fly and that I liked trying/seeing new things long as it were good for me. I did not want anything that would harm me. We sat by the shore just laughing and talking. I did not know if I was really digging him, or if it was the money that I was loving. I just knew that I was attracted to something, and I do not think it was Roe.

When we got back to the hotel, he reached into his glove box to get his checkbook and asked me who should I write the check to. I told him to make it payable to No Room for Dust Foundation. He looked at me and said, "So you don't have any room for foolishness?" I replied, "Now, you are learning." I came up with that name in a matter of seconds and all I had to do was open a business account in that name. He wrote the check out for one-hundred thousand dollars just as he said he would. He thought that I lived in Dallas, Texas and that is the way I was going to keep it. I knew that he was expecting something in return, and I wanted to give it to him. I had to bait that thing and reel the fish in to eat. It was not anything personal, but business.

Now, do not think that I slept around with every baller I met, because I did not. I told you that I liked him and that he had two things going for himself. He was rich, and we clicked. But more so, he was married and had been for over ten years, so I was good. I was not looking for a relationship because I had just come out of one with a woman. (Yes, a woman.) There isn't anything under the sun that I haven't done. However, Jesus saved a wrench like me. I once was lost, but thank God, I'm found. You may have thought that I was horrible and called me every name but a child of God, and that is okay. I believe that I was working on my testimony. You have to go through some stuff to worship God the way I do. I give Him a whoop and holler praise, and I will praise Him for the rest of my days.

I arrived back in Dallas on Sunday morning after having a blast in Miami. Roe was really beginning to blow my cell phone up, and it was beginning to bother me in the worst way. I was thinking that he needed to be with his wife and leave me alone. The next morning, I got up and got things straight for the business. I headed to the bank and opened the business account by depositing that check. I figured I would drag Roe along until the check cleared and I could transfer the funds later. You would have wanted to be a fly on the wall when I broke the news to him that it would soon be over. I did not want him.

He had already told me to be cool, and I could get all the things I wanted. I just had to stay on the sideline until he got the divorce from his wife without her taking him for every dime that he had worked for. Here I was thinking that this fool must think I'm a fool, too. I knew he had the right game, but it was with the wrong female, and I was not the one. I was a stick and move chick that did not want to wipe one person out, so I made my rounds. I was like a thief in the night - in and out. I had to be quick because I was playing on people's intelligence. Moreover, when you mess with someone's money, they get pissed. Therefore, I was like a ghost that vanished.

Ring! Ring! "Hello," I said in a soft voice and trying to stay calm. Roe told me that he wanted me to meet him in Vegas for the weekend. I told him that I could not because I had important meetings all week and that I had just left Miami. I told him that there was no way I could make it. However, if I got all my sponsors in agreeance this week, then the next weekend I would see him even if I had to come to Miami. He was sounding all disappointed. So, I acted as if I hated not being able to meet with him because I wanted to spend time with him just as he wanted to spend time with me. In reality, I was only waiting for that check to clear, and then I would really let him have it.

I was sick of that whining boy. He was definitely not a man acting like that, and it bothered me in the worst way. I was thinking to myself, "*If I was his wife, I would've been gone. But, some women are just as bad.*" I finally told him to save his best for me, and I would see him next weekend. He said, "Okay, I will talk to you later my sexy red thang. I loooov…" Click! I hung the phone up. I cared nothing about love, and especially from someone that was married and had been for a long time. Please! So where did I fit? I fit right in that fool's wallet.

Ten days had passed, and the check cleared. I was really excited because I could fall back on my hustle for a few weeks and spend time with my kids. I would buy them whatever they wanted, and I would take them wherever they choose to go. Although I was in the streets a lot, I did come home to my babies. I had mad love for my kids. I had a boy and a girl, and I felt like God had given me my pair. I would do anything for my kids, and I gave them everything a kid could possibly want.

I called my son my little rider because he was so like me. I thought that if he was like me, then he was really smart. I called my little girl my angel because she was so lame to the game and did everything right. I wondered most of the time if the doctors gave me the wrong child because she was so different. She was simply a good kid, even around the worst of people. She had a light that shined brightly. In honesty, I think she covered us in our mess because she was a praying little girl.

My kids did not know about the stuff I was doing. They had a good father, and he was very active in their lives. Their father was such a good man, and he was a good example for the kids. He worked hard and taught them in the process. He was patiently waiting for me to get it together, but that was not about to happen. He wanted to marry me and settle down, but I was too busy for that. I wanted to just live life the way I wanted, and working hard was not on my list. I did not want to clock in on someone else's clock.

He had my heart in the beginning and messed up. I forgave him but never did forget, and that ended all the love I had for him. I did not like the feeling of being hurt, and I was going to be sure that I did not allow anyone else to invade my space. People only had one time to mess up with me. I was not like Jesus who handed out many chances. That was the way I was, and I thought that was the way I had to be.

Meanwhile, Roe was starting to really get on my nerves. He was blowing my phone up, so I had a trick up my sleeve. I flew to Miami a few times for about two months. and I was fed up because he had fallen in love and was ready to leave his family for me. I waited good until I knew he was home, and I called his phone back to back. He finally answered like he was irritated, and I told him that I wanted him to come be with me that night. He was making every excuse in the book and was trying to make it seem as if it was a business call he was on in front of the wifey.

Roe said to me, "Sam, I will holler back at you tomorrow during business hours." I went off and told him not to ever contact me back. I told him that I was done and I knew where his heart was. I hung up the phone as if I had accomplished a goal. However, Roe called my phone an hour later asking me what was the problem and blah blah blah.

My response was, "Boy, I do not want to hear all the BS. I am just sick and tired of being sick and tired. It's best we just go our separate ways." He was not trying to hear that, but it was beyond time and much longer than I would usually string a person along. Let's just say I was finished, and once again, I had pulled a ghost move on that fool. That throw away cell phone was tossed, and that would be his last call that would reach me.

Chapter Eleven

Sleeping with the Enemy

Life has its way of changing things. Just when you think that you can go on and live life to the fullest, you get knocked right back down. I finally finished the drug program and was headed to the halfway house where I would spend six months. I had plans and a vision. When I got there, I found myself talking to a guy that was attractive to me. Mac was different. I think I liked the way he carried himself. He would go to work, and then he would come in and get ready for the next day. He worked at Calumet as a pipefitter, and he was definitely making a decent amount of money.

I knew that he liked me, and we started getting to know each other and sharing small things about our lives. The relationship progressed, and he started giving me money. That was my way of feeling a sense of entitlement along with assurance. I felt like he could understand and relate with me because he had been in the same situation as myself. I liked Mac, but God did not tell me that he was my Boaz. God did not tell me that this was the man that I was going to marry and spend the rest of my life with. I just assumed this by deceiving myself.

One day, while I was walking to the library, I stumbled up on a lick. A man was trying to talk to me as I was headed back to the halfway house. He ran to me asking for my name and my number. I was thinking that this old man did not have much, but I would soon find out otherwise.

You can never judge a book by the cover, so do not even attempt to do so. I gave him my cell number, and he gave me his. I got back to the halfway house, and after I talking to Mac, I did chores, and showered for the night, I called him. I won't call him by his real name, so I will address him as my sugar daddy. Anyway, I was totally honest with him about who I am and where I was staying. Can you believe that he was okay with that? He told me that he admired my honesty and that he wanted me to come and work for him. I told him that he would have to say that he was my uncle because I did not want Mac to know about the old man that I was about to start using.

My sugar daddy had some doe. He gave me one thousand dollars every Friday. I was saying that God was truly good. However, that was not God because He does not work like this. This was a married man, and I had no intentions to be with him. This man did not know if I was a man or woman. He just enjoyed being in my presence. I clocked in and out the whole time as if I worked for him. He had contracts from the City of Shreveport. He picked me up every day around noon because I was too lazy to get up early like normal people. I would leave around lunch and come back after dinner. I had it made in the shade, and his wife had no idea that her husband was tricking with a young tenderoni. He was the easiest trick that I've ever dealt with, and I could tell him anything.

I did not see any harm in the matter, and I thought it was okay. After all, it was not like we were sexually involved in anyway. He would tell me that he just admired looking at me and called me his angel. Well, I was his angel until he found out about Mac and when I told him that I did not love him like that. I was truthful with him because he had told his wife about me.

He told her that he was in love with someone else. I heard him tell her this, and I know it crushed her because they had been married for over twenty-five years. Then, a young girl comes along and destroys their marriage. I told him that he was foolish for saying those things to his wife because I could never feel for him the way she does. I told him that if he did not pay me like he did, I would be gone. So that is when I became a Jezebel in disguise. He thought the worst of me and said that I was a gold digger. I really did not care because I cared nothing for this man. Let's just say not in the way that he felt for me.

Finally, my time was up for being at the halfway house. I moved in with my dad for about thirty days. Mac and I were really moving quickly in our relationship. I quickly put a demand on him by letting him know that it would be marriage or nothing. That was in January, and we were married in March. I truly pushed him to move faster than he was trying to, but he just did not want a good thing to pass him by. It was not long after that I was pregnant with his child. And, shortly after that, he got laid off from his job. That led to him picking up the bottle and drinking like a fish.

I had no idea who I had married, I realized that I was sleeping with the enemy. This man was assigned by satan. He wanted to kill, steal, and destroy me in the worst way. I was given so many signs from the beginning, and I chose to ignore them all. My dad said no, my kids said no, my friends said no, but I said yes. Nevertheless, I was married and pregnant with his child.

Our life together started getting bad when he lost his job and started drinking. I was shocked because I had never seen him take a drink before and now he is drinking regularly. He would get drunk, and his personality would change. It got so ugly that I thought satan was going to kill me. I would call the cops so much that they wanted to take me in for calling too much. I told them that I would continue to call because they are supposed to serve and protect. I did not feel like I was making false calls. I was simply being careful. I did not know if I would kill him or if he would kill me. I just knew that it was dangerous for the both of us. Nonetheless, I had to make a way of escape, and I needed God to show up and save me.

Now, do not think that I did not try to make my marriage work because I did. I gave 110% and was true to my husband regardless of the way that he treated me. I wanted it to work. We went to counseling with our Bishop, and he would give us assignments to follow and exercises in our marriage to make it work. Still, it just was not working. My daughter was witnessing the verbal abuse when he drank, and she even witnessed the physical abuse once. She had to dial 9-1-1 because he had choked me until I passed out.

I knew that the marriage was over, but I stayed and worked on it for a whole year. I gave him a timeframe to get it together, and he did not. I explained to my kids that this was not the way man and woman are supposed to live. That is hard to explain to a child when you are still in a bad relationship like the one I was suffering. It was hard to breathe in my house, and it was hard to go to sleep at night for not knowing how the enemy would come in. I started sleeping with a butcher knife under my pillow, because I had intentions of slicing Mac into fine pieces whenever he decided to attack. I was ready and that spirit knew it.

I finally got out of the bad situation and was able to move on with my life. I was at peace with being separated. I stayed that way for about four years before I filed for a divorce. I think I stayed that way in hopes that God would save him and maybe we could get back together and restore our marriage. That did not work, and I was okay with that. So, there I was raising another child without a father present daily. On the other hand, I really needed that time alone, and my kids were happy again. I did as I pleased and cooked when I felt like it. I was finally back to my old self, and it felt good. They were happy and that settled me. I had to thank God for saving me once again and I was so glad that He loved me despite my shortcomings.

I really do not want to go on about that season in my life because that chapter is over. I just want to encourage all women that if a man isn't treating you like the queen you are, then leave him alone. Trust me, what one man won't value, the next will treasure. Ladies, they are not worth the heartaches, the pain, nor the headaches. I encourage you to let that no good fool go. My favorite saying is when you walk up to a person doorstep there is a doormat at the front door that says WELCOME. So, I tell each person that enters, you are so welcome to come. But, when they want to switch personalities, I tell them that they are surely welcome to go. I encourage you to wait on your Boaz. God did not want us with a broke-az, a dumb-az, nor a jack-az. The choice is yours.

Chapter Twelve

Life Goes On

To every woman struggling with men issues, I want you to know that you have to be confident in your own self-worth and not be persuaded to believe the foolishness that men try to tell us. They will say anything to keep us stuck. I want you to stop, look in the mirror, and say, "I am all that and some. I am who God created me to be." Trust me, ladies, you are joint heirs of the kingdom. Why do you think that this no good man is there in the first place? He sees and knows your worth. We are every man's help mate. They need us more than they want to admit. You better start seeing your value, and start acting like David by encouraging yourself in the Lord your God.

You may be wondering how do you press through hardship and how do you overcome evil with good? I am telling you that no matter what comes your way, you have to trust that God is going to make a way of escape for you. I want you to prepare yourself, because the adversary is coming equip with all the tools necessary to destroy you. He knows exactly our weak areas and which buttons to press. So, prepare yourself and stay prayed up. Then, when the enemy comes in like a flood, God will raise a standard.

Attack

The devil knows that he cannot get me off the mark when it comes to the way I worship God. He knows that I am sold out and that man cannot tell me anything when it comes to my father. I know that He will never leave me nor forsake me ever. He has been so good to me and better to me than I have been to myself. The enemy knows this and continues to prey on you in hopes that he will last longer than you. Sadly, we tend to forget and that is where he catches us off guard. It's the little foxes and those small cracks that we forget about.

You must always stay in position. You have to read your word daily and exercise your faith on a daily basis. That is why it clearly states in the bible for us to meditate on God's word day in and day out. The key is if we stay focused and stay prayed up, we can stand no matter what comes our way. Remember, the battle has already been won when Jesus died on the cross, took the sting out of death, and rose with all power. Psalm 34:19 says, "many are the afflictions of the righteous: but the Lord delivers him out of them all." I want you to pause and say, "It stops right now."

I have a personal relationship with Him, and I encourage you to draw nigh unto Him. In return, He will draw nigh unto you. Turn from your wicked ways and surrender to Him. Then, He will hear from you. Am I saying that you have to be perfect? No, because there is only one. However, I am saying that you have to sin less. All I am trying to tell you is that many are the afflictions of the righteous, but the Lord delivers him out of them all.

Psalm 34:1 says, "I will bless the Lord at all times.

His praise shall continually be in my mouth." When the doctor gives you a bad report, bless the Lord. When so-called friends turn their backs on you, bless the Lord. When your family gives up on you, bless the Lord. When circumstances seem impossible, bless the Lord. When the enemy comes in like a flood, bless the Lord. I encourage you to bless the Lord at all times.

Chapter Thirteen

A Lady Always Knows When to Excuse Herself

It took me four months to write this book, and to God be the glory. He gave me the vision and the time that I would have to perfect this book. I was able to see the lady that I was sitting with transition into heaven. She was truly a beautiful lady. She lived ninety long years and never complained. I became so close to her that I started calling her grandma and no longer Grandmere as everyone called her. She was such a courageous woman and very soft spoken. She did not talk much. When she did, she used words gracefully. I admired her and I was thankful that God allowed me the opportunity to assist and care for her. I loved her, and I would make jokes that she was my white grandmother. We'd both laugh. I knew she grew to love me back because she showed it. The night before she passed, she wanted me to sleep with her in her bed, and I did.

The next morning, I was assigned to pray on a conference call, and I just wanted her to rest without hearing my mouth. So, I texted my church members and told them that I wouldn't be able to pray and for them to allow someone to take my place. I also asked them to please pray for my lady and informed them that we would be on the call. The group sang and prayed for Grandmere, and after the conference call, she seemed so at peace. I laid there with her quietly, and soon after the call, the doorbell rang. I had forgotten to unlock the door for the next shift. Mary was at the door waiting, and I told Grandmere that I was going to let her in.

I got up and went to unlock the door. When Mary came in, we walked towards the bedroom and I was telling her about our night and that I had slept with Grandmere. I told her how I had comforted her the whole night. When we turned on the light, Grandmere was gone to heaven, and I felt great. My Bishop had just started a series on the right touch, and I knew that I had given her the right touch. I know that I did everything in my might to make her last days peaceful and enjoyable. Her grandson said that a lady always knows when to excuse herself, and I will have to agree with that.

God spoke to me and said, "Job well done. You passed the test. Because of your faithfulness, I am giving you an extension on your life." If only you knew how that felt and how grateful I am. I will bless the Lord at all times, and His praise will continually be in my mouth.

I will leave you with this: Be sure to listen to God even when it doesn't make sense to your flesh. The spirit is always willing, but the flesh will do its own thing. Try to stay in the spiritual realm and know that you can do all things through Christ which strengthens you. You should only trust God and put your confidence only in people, but do not be disappointed when man fails. The bible clearly states that man will let you down every single time. They have good intentions, but they are only human.

Chapter Fourteen

It's Not Over

I struggled getting up one morning, but I had to hurry because I was attending Memories with Mom at school with my baby girl, Hailey. I could not miss because she would scold me, and I did not want that. So, I got out of bed and headed to the shower. My head was hurting really badly, but I pushed forward and continued with preparing myself to head out to the school. It was just around the corner, so it wouldn't take long to get there.

When I arrived, I went to Hailey's classroom and walked with the students to lunch. We got our trays and got seated. I was trying to convince Hailey to eat her food, but she always complains about how bad it is. Therefore, I did not push her to eat. I sat eating quietly because I started getting blurred vision, and I could no longer make out who was who. I had on my glasses so that was not the problem. Her teacher signaled for the class to get up and exit the cafeteria. I remember holding Hailey's hand for guidance, but I did not let her know what was happening.

In my mind, I was screaming, *Jesus NOOOOOOOO*. We walked to her classroom, and I kissed her goodbye. As soon as I exited the room, I reached for the pole and that became my guide. I prayed to God and asked Him to bring my sight back, but it was slowly fading. I continued praying and made it to the truck safely. I sighed in relief. Still, I was crying and asked God to please let me make it to Bishop. His job is right by Hailey's school. I wanted God to guide me there so that he could pray for me. I was like the woman with the issue of blood. If I could just get to Bishop, I knew I would be alright.

I made it to Brookshire's parking lot. He's the store director there and has been with the company thirty plus years. I got out of the truck and made my way inside the store. A lady approached me and asked if I need assistance. I obviously had a look on my face that signaled I was in trouble or perhaps I looked timid. I asked if Bishop was there, and she guided me to his office. His words to me were, "Daughter, what is wrong?" I remember breaking down in tears and falling into his arms saying, "I cannot see. My vision is leaving me."

He immediately started praying for me. He told me that this was an attack from the enemy and that I would be okay. My vision was still blurry but my faith senses had kicked in, and God led me to the house safely. "Thank you, Jesus" was all I could say when I pulled up to the house. I called my husband, still afraid because I could no longer see again. He came home as I was lying in bed. My head was still throbbing, so we called my doctor. He wanted me to come in right away. They immediately did an MRI on my brain, but I was not thinking anything bad. So, we went home and returned the next day for the results.

I can remember vividly both doctors walking into the room to tell my husband and me that I had brain cancer and that I had seventeen tumors around my brain stem. Three of the tumors were large like lemons and my condition was gravely. They told me that they were not sure what the radiation doctor would say, but that they were admitting me into the hospital. I looked at my husband and started crying. They wanted to excuse us to give us privacy and time to talk, so they left the room.

I felt so much hurt because I had just survived Stage IV breast cancer and was doing really great. Now God had allowed the enemy to throw another dart my way. To me, it seemed like the devil had hit the bullseye right in the middle. As for my husband, he seemed to be taking it better than I could ever. I suppose he had become numb after going through such tragedy. To me this was totally uncommon. This was my brain, and I had seventeen tumors on it. I wanted to just die right then and there. The enemy is really crafty and has so many tactics. He wants us to lose our hope and die. I asked my husband what he thought, and he was upset as well. I think he was more hurt than upset, but it seemed to me that he was angry with God. That is when my faith kicked into gear, and I told him that God has another testimony for me.

A nurse wheeled me to my room. I have to admit, I was definitely heart broken. I laid there in disbelief, but it was real. The radiation doctor showed up and asked if my vision was still gone and the answer was yes. He then went on to tell me that I had too many tumors on my brain to have surgery and that I wouldn't live if they tried. He said it in a nice way by saying it was gravely. They believed that if they did surgery, it would cause more harm, than help. He did not want to take the risk, but he would give me five radiation treatments at the max on what could be given.

I was so hurt because I was wondering why was not this discovered before now and why did they not catch this sooner? I have always made my appointments and all my CT Scans. Why did they miss it? I asked if everyone could leave me alone because I needed to speak to God alone, and I needed some answers. They left at my request and that is when I flopped back onto the bed really hard and yelled out, "WHAT NOW GOD?" I felt defeated, and He told me to get up and walk to the bathroom. I did as I was told. When I got to the bathroom, He instructed me to look in the mirror. I did, but my vision was slightly there.

He asked what did I see, and I asked what He meant.

He asked again, "What do you see?"
I said, "I see me."
He asked me what did I look like.
I said, "What do you mean?"
He then asked, "How do you look?"
"How do I look? I look like me."
"And, how do you look?"
"I look good!"

"So, why are you complaining?" God said. "You look the way you do because I am carrying you. You do not look like what you are going through. So, why are you complaining? It's me who gives life and everything that has happened concerning your life has always been major. You have never experienced minor in anything. So, why give up now? You have always put your trust in me, and I want you to trust me now. I made you! I am your God, and you are my daughter. I will keep you in perfect peace, but you must stay focused.

"I am bigger than your sickness. I am bigger than cancer. I am bigger than your infirmities and I am bigger than the universe. You asked, 'What now?' Trust me, and I will carry you. You shall live. This battle has already been won. By my stripes, you are already healed. I want you to walk in it no matter how you feel, no matter what the doctors tell you, and no matter what others say. You have to stand." I went back to my bed with a sigh of relief, and I knew God was right. Thank you, Jesus. I was about to work on my next testimony.

My sisters bombarded the hospital room. My oldest (Tina) became my angel and the twins (Aisha & Kasheka) have always been tight. They drove from Texas out of fear, and I had to encourage them that I would be okay and that God was prepping me for my next testimony. The next day, the nurse wheeled me to radiation, and I hung in there like a champ. The procedure seemed easy and did not seem like it would be too hard or complicated for me. On day two, I felt the same way. However, on day three, I felt like I was sinking in a river and could no longer swim. I was definitely in the deep end, and I was drowning.

The radiation had the best of me. On day four, I was reluctant about going. I was upset when I did. I started eating less, and my head was hurting. I felt weak, and I was barely walking. All my strength was diminishing slowly, and I was aware. I would get home and sleep the day away and then the night. I was conformed to my bed, and the hours became days and the days became months. I was slipping away, and I had not picked up my bible at all. I had not read my word at all, and I had started missing church. I was too sick to go, and I did not have the strength.

I was glad that radiation would be closed for the Christmas holidays because that would give me time to be revived a little before getting the last treatment. I thought I would feel better, but it got worse. I WAS WEAK! Christmas came and went, and I woke up early that morning so that I could watch my girls open their gifts. I was trying so hard to be in the Christmas spirit, which was hard because of my condition.

After they opened their gifts, I got back in bed and slept. On Monday, my family had to literally drag me to radiation because I did not want to go. I started throwing up some foods, and each day became a nightmare. I did my last radiation treatment in anger, but I did it. The techs were really nice because they talked to me with sincerity, and they were always kind. I think they felt that I was going to die and that it was pointless on getting those treatments with so many tumors crowding my brain.

The doctor came in and asked if my sight was back, and it was still blurry. I had prayed and asked God please do not do me like Saul. I asked Him to please restore my sight. PLEASE GOD was all I could scream. I went home and back to bed I went. I was depressed, and I felt like life was over for me. My kids, my parents, and my husband all saw me slipping away. My pastor's wife saw me like this, and I no longer wanted her seeing me in that state. My cousins, Hope and Imani, came even when I did not want them to, and I was miserable.

I told everyone that I was miserable, and it was not because I had no hope. It was just because that was how I felt. I did not want to lie to myself or anyone else, so I spoke the truth. I had lots of visitors invading my privacy. They came praying for me, and I knew some of the prayers were not reaching heaven. The bible says, "we know the spirit by the spirit." I knew, but I let them pray only because they said Jesus' name.

I was back and forth from the hospital to my bedroom. I was going back and forth to get fluids in me, because I was still not able to hold anything down. I was weak in spirit, and I was physically exhausted. I barely was able to walk, and it got harder day by day.

One night, I was sleeping and the enemy tried killing me. He came in the image of my husband, which is very tall. That spirit hovered over me mimicking my husband. Now, Sederick kisses me each morning before going to work. So, this spirit kissed me on the forehead. Then, it covered my head and pinned me down. I was suffocating and could not breathe. I was too weak to break free, and I called on Jesus. That is when he went into my closet and vanished.

You may think that I was dreaming, but I was very much awake. I screamed Sederick's name as I reached for him at three o'clock in the morning. He awakened startled to see what was the matter. I told him the devil had just tried to take me out and acted as if it was him. I had him to get up and turn the bathroom light on because I refused to go back to sleep in the dark. He even thought that I had a bad dream, but I was well aware of what had just happened. The next day, I started talking crazy about death. I started telling my mom that I want to be cremated and how I wanted my funeral to be. I wanted it short and sweet and not a lot of people. I wanted my pastor's wife to do the eulogy, and I knew she would sing a sweet song that would be meaningful. I was ready to DIE…

That night I fell asleep with my husband beside me. The devil tried to take me out again. This time, he did not try to kiss me. He just covered my head and began to smother me like he did the night before. I repeat, I had no strength to fight or defend myself at all. I was totally defenseless, but God stepped in, and I rose above the covers gasping for air. I was very afraid, and my husband was awake trying to comfort me. However, he still thought it was a bad dream. I knew it was not, and I knew the enemy was trying to take me out. I had no spiritual food nor did I have any nutritional food either. This was a battle that I wanted to give up on, but God wouldn't allow me.

My dad came over the next morning, and I told him what had transpired over the two days. He listened attentively and saw death in my eyes. I want you to know that my dad is a praying man. He knows God and has a relationship with him, so I knew he understood what I had told him. He knew the devil was trying to take me out. My dad left the room with his head hanging down. He did not have the posture of a saint that was close to God, but he had the posture and look of a wounded dad that loved his child so much. You could see the hurt in his walk, you could hear the hurt in his talk, and you could see the hurt that was piercing from his heart and soul. My dad was covered in anguish.

The next day, my mom came into my bedroom and laid with me. She cried, and there was nothing I could do. I could not pour any word in her because the devil had zapped me, and I was delusional. I was not myself at all. She told me that she needed to get away and go to Texas for the weekend just to get a break from all this. She told me she needed to come to grips that I was dying. It was so hard, and I could see it in her eyes. Still, there was nothing I could do or say.

This has been a trying year for me. My son was sentenced to twenty-five years for a crime he did not commit, but he decided to take a plea bargain so I wouldn't have to come to court any longer. They were trying to give me five years if found guilty. My son refused and took a plea to drop all charges against me.

I was so devastated, but there was nothing I could do because he took the deal without telling me first. I was so pissed at his attorney because she had allowed him to do it and did not notify me beforehand of what had transpired. I was furious because I had paid thousands of dollars for her to represent him well. It's not over is all I will say. When God tells you something, trust that and continue to go forward. Joshua 3:3 says, "When you see the ark of the covenant of the Lord your God and the priests, the Levites bearing it, then you shall remove from your place and go after it."

I think we should all trust the process. God made us in His own likeness, and He created the heaven and the earth. Why is it so hard to trust our daddy that created all, made all, and knows all? That is crazy but it is real. My mom packed her bags and left that Sunday. My dad came into my room and started speaking word to me. He told me stories in the bible that I knew, and he told me scriptures that I had remembered.

Little did I know, he was reviving my spirit man. I started thinking more clearly, and I could see a dim light at the end of a tunnel. My dad paced that floor for nearly three hours without stopping to rest for anything. He was fervent and determined. He said that day was the day that I would be revived, and the devil who almost won had to flee. He was speaking life back into my limp body. He nourished me spiritually, and my heart was filled with gratitude.

My dad had not given up on me, and he surely had not given up on God. He was standing in the gap for me and waiting on God to manifest in the flesh. He stated, God would show evidence because He has never seen the righteous forsaken nor His seed begging for bread. Then, Hailey walked into the room wanting to go to the corner store for candy. My dad told me he would take her and that he would be right back, and they went to the Circle K.

As I laid there, the spirit prompted me to get out of the bed. I walked over to the dresser and picked my bible up. That bible was extremely heavy, and it weighed me down. After all, I was weak and barely standing from lack of food and word. Still, I began walking down the hall quoting Psalm 23, "the Lord is my shepherd, and I shall not want. He makes me lie down in green pastures. He leads me beside the still waters. He restores my soul." Then, I began saying, "DO IT GOD! DO IT GOD! Build me back up. I am weak, and I need your strength. Please forgive me God for forgetting who you are and who I belong to. Forgive me!"

As I turned around in the hall to press on and move forward, I said, "It is you who restores my soul. Please lead me in the path of righteousness for your name's sake. Yea though I walk through the valley of the shadow of death, I will fear no evil." I started worshipping God as I was pacing back and forth through the hallway. "DO IT GOD! For you are with me, thy rod and thy staff comfort me. You have prepared a table before me in the presence of my enemies and you have anointed my head with oil. My cup is running over. Surely goodness and mercy shall follow me all the days of my life and I will dwell in the house of the Lord forever."

My Pastor Bishop J. Anthony Grant and his queen Co-Pastor Elder Angela Grant walked in the house. Co-

Pastor said to me, "Look at you." I turned around, and she said, "I'm proud of you for having your bible in hand." I gave a slight laugh and told her that this was the first time in two months that I had picked it up. I told her that was why I had not been to church; the devil had been winning. They both told me that was ok and what is important was that I had gotten up.

The devil cannot keep a warrior down. Speaking of which, that is how my hair started growing back in a Mohawk. People thought that was the way I cut it, and I told them that was simply the way it had grown. Bishop said that I had my war look. I looked it up, and it said that it symbolized who they were and that they were called the Pawnee which were great warriors. I believe that this was my fight to war with the devil to defeat him and put him under my feet.

Bishop prayed over all my medication that I had a problem with taking, and he told me to start taking them right away. I said, "But, they make me throw up." He said, "Do you trust me?" I said I did, and he told me to take the meds. He said it would be different this time. He said he had prayed for me in the spiritual and it would work in the spiritual realm. He told me that I would take my meds, and I would begin eating and drinking again. I thought, *"Oh boy, I have to step out on faith."* I agreed with a nod, and they left saying they love me and they would be back to check on me.

I felt much better but my stomach was empty. I began eating, and I was still throwing up. However, I ignored it and kept trying anyhow. The next few days were not as bad. I was still throwing up, but I'm consistently in my word each day. I was starting to feel a little better in my body. I sent Co-Pastor a text telling her that I was still throwing up. She replied that the Bishop said if I do not quit, it will quit. So, I soaked that in and kept eating and drinking. I did not quit and guess what? It quit! Wow! God is amazing.

I am closer to Christ now more than I've ever been. I wake up to Jesus and I go to bed to Jesus. I know now that I will not live without Christ and that for me to live, I have to eat daily. Yes, physically but I'm also talking about spiritual food. I have been studying to live, and I preach what I live. I thank God for having a God conscience now in everything I do. It's all about Christ and His purpose for our lives. We just need to move when God says to do so. I attend church on Sunday and then on Wednesday for bible class. I am back in place and flowing in the spirit. I see what I could not see, and I am operating as God speaks to me. I lay in bed in the mornings just to rest in His bosom. I wait long enough to hear His voice to command me what to do today. It's amazing when we can rest in God knowing all is well.

One month after my breakthrough began, I had to go and get an MRI done to see what the tumors were doing. I felt like I was healed because I could see fully again. The headaches had diminished, and I was feeling like my old self. I felt like in all my praise and worship, I was being healed. My kids' grandmother (Momma Fannie) called me one morning and said that God told her to quit praying for my healing and that He already healed me. God told her to pray for my strength and to pray for my faith. I knew that day I was healed. I stood on that, and I believed every word.

My daughter (Je'Sika) who attends University of Arkansas at Pine Bluff had completed the semester with honors. I am so godly proud of her. She did well through all of this, and she stood tall. She is definitely a survivor and has the drive to complete any task that is been given. After that semester, she drove home for a week since school was out. She showed up just in time for me to go and get my results from the MRI. While waiting for the doctor, I told her that I needed for her to start recording when the doctor comes in. The doctor came in and gave me a good report. All seventeen of my tumors are completely gone! Oh, my God, it felt good because my God had done it again!

I got home and started sending texts out to all my family members. I knew that some of them wouldn't believe. They would feel like it was me just me stepping out on faith once again and that the doctors had not given me that report. This was the reason I had Je'Sika recording. I knew God healed me, and I knew the doctor would give that report. Why would I have her to record bad news? This time, I would have proof for all the unbelievers. I have a cousin who's a doctor, and she doesn't believe - at least not like I do. She does everything from the medical standpoint. So, I texted the recordings to her. That is when she told me that she was glad she heard the doctor's report, and she believed me then. Wow! Oh, ye of little faith. When man says no, God says yes. All you need is one yes, because you will get a thousand no's. I encourage you to keep the faith and hold on to God's unchanging word. If God said it, He's able to perform it. If God said it, He will do it. Line up and receive the promises.

In addition to this book, I encourage you to read my book, *15 Days of Faith*, so that you can tap into and grow the seed that God gave each of us. My prayer is that everyone that has read this book will be able to move mountains and that you will be equipped with power to heal all manner of sickness and disease. I hope that *15 Days of Faith* will be inspiring, motivating, uplifting, and will help push you into your place of purpose and promise. God loves you and that is the reason you have read this book. No worries! As for myself, I am not perfect, but I am limited edition. Until next time, trust God.

About the Author

Erica "Joy" Mathews is a native of Shreveport, Louisiana. She is a loving wife and wonderful mother of three children. The name "Joy" describes her well, and it shows through the love that she bestows upon everyone she meets. She found Christ in 2004. Through her passion in prison ministry and her love for God and others, she has led many to Christianity. She is a member of the Greater New Zion FGBC of Shreveport, LA where she is a minister and remains faithful, fervent, and focused in her walk with Christ.

She received her Associates Degree at Southern University of Shreveport in 2002. This phenomenal entrepreneur woman has owned an array of businesses, and she is an active author, motivational speaker, and business consultant. Joy's strong will, sophistication, and drive will push you into purpose. Her undeniable faith, passion, and belief that with God all things are possible led her to write her debut books ***The devil Almost Won, But God…*** and ***15 Days of Faith***.

Visit www.amazon.com/author/joymathews and www.joymathews.com for purchases.

For booking, visit www.joymathews.com/contact.

www.ingramcontent.com/pod-product-compliance
Lightning Source LLC
Chambersburg PA
CBHW070307100426
42743CB00011B/2381